# BUS & COACH PRES

## A CONCISE GU_ _

*by John A. Godwin*

Brewin Books

First published
by Brewin Books, Studley, Warwickshire, B80 7LG
in September 1995

ISBN 1 85858 039 0


British Library Cataloguing in Publication Data.
A Catalogue record for this book is available from the British Library


Typeset in Garamond and Printed by
Heron Press, Kings Norton, Birmingham B38 9TS

# TABLE OF CONTENTS

# DISCLAIMER NOTICE

During the compilation of this book, much reference has been made to reference publications and to authoritative individuals and organisations in an attempt to ensure a high degree of accuracy. No responsibility of any kind will be accepted by the author or publishers of this volume in the event of any loss, damage or injury of any sort. Before undertaking any mechanical or bodywork restoration, any queries or safety concerns should be addressed to an authoritative professional for clarification. Any uncertainty with regard to legal matters, including driver and vehicle licensing, should be referred either to the D.V.L.A. at Swansea, or to your Local Vehicle Licensing Office (LVLO).

# ACKNOWLEDGMENTS

My grateful thanks for assistance in the compilation of this publication are due to a number of people. First and foremost to my good friend David Gladwin for the hours he spent examining, defacing and improving the proof scripts. My colleagues in the British Bus Preservation Group have supplied much of the practical advice that can only be gained by years of experience. Finally my wife Penny and the tolerant family should not be forgotten, for without their patience to my many hours behind the word processor and on the telephone, this book would not exist !

John A Godwin, Merstham, Surrey. May 1995

# THE CONCISE GUIDE TO BUS AND COACH PRESERVATION

## INTRODUCTION

Tens of thousands of buses and coaches regularly provide an essential service to the British travelling public. Any person who is familiar with this means of transport, whether as a passenger or as an interested observer, will be aware of occasional vehicle improvements which will have upgraded the comfort of journeys and hopefully increased the service reliability. But what has become of all the passenger carrying vehicles of years past that offered a stately style of transport at a relaxing pace ?

Sadly, many of these early milestones in the history of the road passenger transport industry have been lost forever. Perhaps it is for this reason that so many individuals have been encouraged to turn their interest in these vehicles into action, by saving examples of buses and coaches which would otherwise not have survived. Today's bus and coach preservation movement is home to many thousands of vehicles, and this leisurely pursuit is attracting an increasing number of new participants each year.

This publication has been compiled to be a concise, factual volume which an intending newcomer to the world of historic bus and coach preservation can read in its entirety, and thereafter use as a valuable source of reference. Both novices and experts alike are guided through chapters on vehicle choice and availability, how to purchase and collect a historic bus, how to undertake mechanical and bodywork restoration in a methodical manner, and most importantly the gaining of an understanding of the legal complications that preserved bus ownership entails.

Five informative appendices detail the information contained in vehicle registrations, the names and addresses of relevant government departments, a comprehensive list of museums, societies and groups, details of the country's main vehicle dealers and breakers, as well as an example of the financial costs of one year's vehicle ownership. Also included is a chapter which gives a little of the history and suitability of ten of the most popular vehicles chosen for preservation, as well as a summary of the availability of spares.

A publication on this subject (which research has shown as being long overdue) will not only serve to increase awareness of the activities of both individual preservationists and national groups, but hopefully convince the casual enthusiast that the rescuing, restoration and rallying of historic vehicles is a real possibility when they are shown just how easy it is !

# Chapter 1

## WHY DO PEOPLE PRESERVE BUSES ?

Motor buses and coaches have been plying for trade throughout this country for nearly a century, and they have changed quite significantly in that time. The early examples were hand built in Great Britain, finished with high quality wood and fabric trim, and painted in stately colours with elaborate gold fleet names. Today's vehicles are generally mass-produced in factories all over Europe, finished with vandal-proof plastic, and display multi-coloured corporate liveries disguising any individuality that may have existed. How times have changed....

There are a large number of individuals who like to remember the road passenger transport industry as it was in yesteryear. Whilst the buses and coaches may not have been as reliable as their modern day counterparts, they were often hand-built by craftsmen to a higher standard. Some of these individuals even go so far as to provide an active retirement for these relics of our transport heritage, spending every spare moment attending to mechanical adjustments and polishing their pride and joy.

The private preservation of buses and coaches started as recently as the middle of the 1950s. A small group of bus enthusiasts attempted to purchase an elderly double-deck AEC from London Transport in 1955, but the asking price of £100.00 was too great and this vehicle was subsequently scrapped. In 1956, however, the same group located and successfully purchased a 1929 AEC Regal still owned by London Transport that had survived long after other members of the class had been withdrawn. T31 (registration UU 6646), carrying a London General Omnibus Company (LGOC) 30 seat rear entrance body, was the first bus to be successfully acquired by private individuals, and the great publicity which appeared in the national press served to encourage similar-minded individuals in the belief that their dreams could become reality. T31 is still preserved today in original condition, and has just been acquired by the London Bus Preservation Trust.

There were approximately 8,000 known preserved buses and coaches in the United Kingdom in 1993. The majority of these are owned by individual preservationists or preservation groups, whilst others are owned by the successor companies to their original operators or by museums. The hobby of providing a secure future to such vehicles is one that demands a high level of commitment and responsibility: weekends of dismantling and reassembling old and oily mechanical parts, countless hours with assorted paint brushes, an eternity with a miscellany of lubricants and polishes - why do so many people partake in this pastime ?

The magnetic appeal of this unusual interest is three-fold. Firstly, owning an elderly bus is a leisurely pursuit with no fixed timescales and no particularly defined way of achieving an end result. Secondly, their is a great deal of satisfaction to be gained from exhibiting the end-product of your countless hours of labour to thousands of interested and enthusiastic visitors on a rally field. Finally, vehicle owners can often feel totally responsible for the continued existence of their vehicle, knowing that their piece of transport heritage may have been saved from certain destruction by the scrapman's torch.

And when you consider how some individuals spend their spare time - firing balls of paint at each other as they run through woodland, or jumping several hundred feet from the top of a crane with an elastic band around their ankles - then it all seems to be rather relaxed and civilised .....

*Chapter 2*

# WHAT SORT OF VEHICLES ARE CHOSEN
# FOR PRESERVATION ?

When an individual decides to take on the responsibility of owning and maintaining a piece of road transport history, there will be certain types of vehicles that will be more appealing to him than others. Some people will choose a vehicle because of its historical connection, for example it may have been used by a long-since departed municipal fleet where that person lived when he was younger: a Welshman may choose an AEC Regent V from the fleet of Ponytpridd UDC, whereas a Mancunian may settle upon a Salford Leyland Titan. Alternatively, there may be a certain make or type of vehicle that is deemed to be particularly attractive or very unusual, or one that has a very reliable mechanical history such as London Transport's ubiquitous Park Royal bodied AEC Routemaster. Prior experience of preserving buses may be an important factor - there are a number of bus-owning individuals whose collection is specifically confined to only one type of vehicle - the author's own collection comprises of Bedford mini-coaches, each bodied by a different coachworks.

Whilst to the untrained eye the difference between a bus and coach is often indistinguishable - especially on older single-deck vehicles - this too can be an important decision that has to be made before acquiring a vehicle that may be owned and looked after for many years. If you have your heart set on a large double-deck Birmingham Guy Arab with an open platform, your journeying will probably be slow and noisy, and quite cold during the winter months. An AEC Reliance coach from the fleet of Maidstone & District, however, will probably not be as distinctive and noticeable as an Eastern Counties Bristol Lodekka, but the seating will be more comfortable, it should travel at a faster speed and it will probably have a heater that may even work ! Owners of convertible or permanent open-top double deck vehicles (such as the Queen Mary class of Leyland Titans delivered to Southdown in the mid 1960s, or the Sea Dog class of Leyland Atlanteans operated by Devon General) take an even bigger risk with the elements: it can take the best part of a day and much specialist equipment to remove or replace a roof, and these individuals have tended to acquire significant weather forecasting skills as a result!

You need not be limited by the vehicles on offer in the British Isles. A small number of preservationists have such a preference for foreign buses and coaches that they have gone so far as to import their ideal subject ! Very few countries extend as much enthusiasm to the retention and restoration of passenger carrying vehicles as the British, so it is often possible to acquire a wide variety of continental buses at very reasonable prices: although the cost of transporting and importing may weigh the scales against such a scheme. Several Belgian Vetra Berliet and German Henschel trolleybuses have already been secured for continued preservation by British owners, and an occasional early French Renault and Peugeot are also known to exist. The North West Transport Museum has an AEC Regent III on display - it carries a Commonwealth Engineering body and was new to the municipal fleet of Sydney, Australia. There are areas of the world where exiled British buses suitable for preservation still survive - the islands of Malta and Gozo, for example, are well known for their continual operation of assorted single-deck buses from the 1940s and 50s.

The choice, however, does not stop at buses and coaches. There are several hundred preserved trolleybuses in existence, and these require a different set of skills altogether. Aside from the presence of an electric motor instead of a conventional engine, trolleys were equipped with one or two roof-mounted conductors to connect with the overhead electric current supply, and all but the earliest examples were equipped with batteries so that they could travel short distances independently. Trolleys were phased out during the 1950s and 60s as the conventional motor bus became more popular, and the last service was operated in Bradford in 1972. Today's preserved trolleybus needs access to one of the few surviving operational overhead networks if it is to run again, and this will have a large influence on where the trolley is kept. Fortunately, there are a few locations where preserved trolleys can operate under their own electric power, including the Sandtoft Transport Centre near Doncaster, the East Anglia Transport Museum near Lowestoft and the Black Country Museum at Dudley in the West Midlands. If you intend acquiring a trolley, the choice in this country will be limited to those already owned in a preservation capacity. There are, however, a few countries in Europe where this mode of transport is still actively operated, and you may wish to look overseas for one.

Cut-down buses that have become towing wagons (such as former Midland Red LC9-class Leyland Leopards) and other service vehicles are continually popular - not only are they a alternative concept from owning a standard bus, but there is a functional (and possibly money-earning) side to their ownership. Other service fleet vehicles that help to depict bygone bus operations are also a possibility for restoration. The Cobham Bus Museum in Surrey, for example, possesses a London Transport Bedford-Scammell tractor unit with a staff canteen trailer, a mechanical garage floor sweeper, and a converted AEC Regal IV bus as a towing and recovery vehicle.

Age of vehicles is not a deciding factor to today's preservation movement. Until quite recently, it was frowned upon if a rally entrant did not have an exposed radiator and an open platform, although that has happily now been rectified. With the fast turnaround of vehicle stock in the modern bus and coach industry, preservationists have realised that there are many vehicles which have not yet reached their 20th birthday that are in imminent danger of being lost forever. There

*Bus preservationists do not only preserve buses! This line-up of London Transport auxiliary vehicles contains breakdown tenders an emergency equipment store, and a control centre!*

is a current trend of rescuing ECW-bodied Bristol REs, and some individuals are currently taking possession of early Leyland Nationals, Atlanteans and Bristol VRs as their useful days draw to a close. A practical possibility for the first-time preservationist might be to acquire an early Carlyle-bodied Sherpa minibus from the mid 1980s: such a vehicle will be cheap to purchase, benefit from an abundant spares supply and the compact size will make it easy to work on. These minibuses are fast disappearing as newer models become available, and they have a significant place in transport history as part of the de-regulated bus industry minibus revolution !

As can be seen from the above, nearly all buses and coaches are suitable for preservation, as a trip to almost any vehicle gathering up and down the country will show you. But is does not matter whether you are considering acquiring a Gilford of the 1920s or a Daimler Fleetline from the 1970s, the ownership of a large bus or coach is a serious commitment that will demand large quantities of your time and money if you are to succeed.

*Chapter 3*

# BEFORE YOU LOOK FOR YOUR PRIDE AND JOY ...

You will probably already have some idea of what sort of vehicle you are looking for. It may be an antique first operated by the municipality in the town in which you were born, it may be the coach you went to school on, or it may be that you want something so unusual that it is the last survivor of its type. A number of practical constraints now come into play, which will either support your ideas, or force you to think again.

The most important factor throughout your life as a bus and coach preservationist is money. To seriously consider acquiring a piece of our transport heritage, you will have had to set aside an initial sum of money to finance your purchase. At the time of writing (1995), a selection of vehicles suitable for preservation were available in the following price ranges:

| | | | |
|---|---|---|---|
| SINGLE DECK: | Bristol RE | £800 - | £3000 |
| | AEC Regal IV | £1500 - | £4000 |
| | Bedford J2 | £500 - | £4000 |
| | Leyland Leopard | £600 - | £3000 |
| | | | |
| DOUBLE DECK: | Bristol Lodekka | £800 - | £2700 |
| | AEC Regent III | £1500 - | £8000 |
| | AEC Routemaster | £2000 - | £5000 |
| | Leyland Titan PD3 | £800 - | £2500 |

So it is easy to see that different types of vehicle are deemed to be more valuable than others, and that the price range between good and bad examples can stretch to several thousand pounds. It is worth remembering, however, that whilst a good condition vehicle will cost more in initial investment, a cheaper alternative will probably cost as much (if not more) in time and materials spent on its restoration. No matter what end of the price spectrum you decide to enter at, be fully aware that the purchase price of any vehicle will be only the thin end of a very large wedge.

If you are not able to fully fund the purchase of a bus or coach on your own, it may be possible to enter into a partnership with another person(s) to share the costs. partnerships can work very well if planned beforehand that each party will carry out equal amounts of work, and all bills and rent will be split accordingly, although it is in everyone's interest to document the precise partnership details before the vehicle is acquired. It is a sad fact that even those partnerships that had concise prior arrangements have fallen apart after only a short period of time due to differences of opinion amongst the partners.

Alternatively, if your financial situation does not allow the purchase of a bus or coach, then there are a numbers of groups and societies that allow individuals with little capital to become actively involved in the restoration and rallying of historic vehicles without the financial responsibilities of sole ownership. The Maidstone & District and East Kent Bus Club, for example, collectively own a number of vehicles from those fleets which members are encouraged to become involved with. Similarly, the British Bus Preservation Group has several rescued vehicles which require attention, and members are welcome to assist in any way they possibly can.

Before making a purchase, you may wish to consider the possibility of sponsorship for your bus. If you are buying direct from an operator, the promise of retaining the original fleet name and livery may reduce the purchase price. Alternatively, approach the first operator of your vehicle and try to assess whether they would be willing to assist you in the restoration of the vehicle to its original condition. Authentic period advertisements for local businesses (which were traditionally painted on) could be re-applied if a satisfactory agreement can be reached with the proprietors. A few simple enquiries such as these could possibly save you many pounds !

The vehicle that you intend to purchase will also be restricted to those that you are permitted to drive on your driving licence. For further details, see the chapter The Law and Your Vehicle. Basically, there is little point in acquiring a bus that you will not be able to drive when preserved, unless you have the funds available to upgrade your driving licence - about £1000 at 1995 prices - and the confidence that you will pass !

Further expense will be incurred in the storage of your vehicle. Unless you own a very large garden, an empty warehouse or you are a farmer with spare barns available, locating a suitable storage space for your bus is likely to be one of the most difficult problems to solve. It will be easier to house your 29-seat Bedford OB than your 14' high Leyland PD3, especially if you are seeking undercover accommodation, and this may well influence the choice of vehicle you are considering buying.

Most preservationists, however, are forced to accept some form of open-air storage, whether that be a corner of a field, a farmyard, or an industrial yard. If a vehicle is particularly elderly, or in such a poor condition that it would be severely damaged by exposed storage, the intending preservationist would be well advised to persevere and locate suitable undercover accommodation. The best way to locate suitable storage is to make your need known, place advertisements in local newspapers, farmers' magazines, rural village stores shop windows, etc. It may even be worth contacting your local bus museum, although you will probably end up on the end of a long waiting list as nearly all museums are currently already oversubscribed. Even if you are successful in acquiring a slot in a museum, space is usually at such a premium that there may be little room in which to work, and extracting your vehicle may necessitate the removal of dozens of others first ! The price you will pay for your storage will of course vary greatly - in 1995, an open field would not cost more than about £10.00 per bus week, whilst some bus companies who use corners of depots for this purpose have been known to charge more than three times that amount !

Wherever your vehicle ends up, it should be in a location that can offer a high degree of security. Vandalism and theft to vehicles on unsecure, open sites from uninvited visitors has unfortunately lead to the untimely demise of many preserved buses: whilst it takes a social outcast less than a minute to break all of your vehicle's windows, it will cost you many hundreds of pounds to achieve their replacement - paying a little extra for a secure store will be a worthwhile investment. Your storage should also ideally offer running water (which is necessary for the restoration and running of your bus), and electricity (for lighting and the use of power tools).

Have some pre-formed idea in your mind about your own vehicle restoration capabilities. If your experience is limited, it will be a wiser investment to acquire a bus which requires only minimal attention, and is more or less ready to rally. Many intending preservationists have started work on vehicles only to find that a lack of expertise leads to a decline in enthusiasm and the project is abandoned. Many potentially historic vehicles have sadly been lost through serious neglect this way.

The intending preservationist should also consider whether he is suitably equipped for the many tasks he will have to undertake. An essential requirement for all but the simplest maintenance is a comprehensive tool-kit. Aside from a socket set, set of spanners and assorted screwdrivers, tools such as pliers, clamps, hammers, chisels and a hacksaw will be frequently utilised. Don't overlook the fact that your modern kit of metric spanners will probably be of no use to a pre-1970 vehicle - you may have to locate and acquire a set of Imperial or Whitworth measurement tools. You will require access to a hydraulic jack which can safely lift your vehicle (check loading capacities carefully) for wheel changes, etc, and also a wheel brace with significant leverage to remove wheel nuts. Other hardware such as an electric drill, a box sander and an extension cable will also be required. Whilst much of the above may already be owned by the enthusiastic mechanic, these items will be a necessary investment in caring for your public service vehicle.

Finally, be aware that whilst it would be satisfying and unusual to own a unique vehicle that is one of the last survivors of its type, the problems associated with such rarities can cause all sorts of nightmares for the owner. spares availability should be carefully checked (many specialist societies and clubs hold sources of commonly required parts), and if stocks are low or non-existent, be fully prepared for extremely long searches for high-priced parts, or expensive bills for specially commissioned replacement components.

*Chapter 4*

## LOCATING THE VEHICLE OF YOUR CHOICE

There are several different methods by which vehicles can be located for preservation. By far the easiest way to be kept informed of available historic buses and coaches is to join one of the specialist societies - such as the Historic Commercial Vehicle Society or the British Bus Preservation Group - and study the classified columns of their respective magazines. Not only will membership of such organisations assist your search for a suitable subject, but it will also allow you to make some useful contacts which may prove invaluable during the course of your restoration. Regional Auto-Trader and Exchange & Mart periodicals occasionally contain a small selection of buses and coaches, but these are rarely of any significant historical interest to the preservationist. Recent times have seen such entries submitted by trade sources, and the genuine bargains are hardly ever advertised by these means.

You may prefer to see a selection of available vehicles first hand, and to this end, it will be necessary to travel to the premises of dealers and breakers (addresses of which are given later). This is particularly useful if you are considering the purchase of a more modern vehicle (1960 onwards), because many examples from this era are still resident in yards up and down the country. Some enthusiast magazines such as Autobus Review Publication's "Bus Fayre" regularly detail which vehicles are currently resident at the main dealers' premises, and this information should assist you in deciding where to go. If you are travelling a long distance on your shopping trip, it would be a good idea to telephone the proprietors first to ensure that they will be open and will allow you to visit.

If the make of vehicle that you wish to acquire is comparatively modern, then it is possible that an example will still be in regular service with an operator. To a preservationist, this could present an opportunity to acquire a running example that has been well maintained on a regular basis, although the price may be significantly higher than an equivalent vehicle at the local breaker's yard. If such a vehicle can be located, it will be worthwhile registering your interest with the current owner, and seeking an indication of when it may be withdrawn from use and available for onward disposal.

A final option in your quest for ownership is that of scouring the hedgerows of the countryside in an attempt to re-discover a long lost vehicle. The advent of bus preservation in the 1950s and 60s saw many neglected vehicles being rescued from obscure and often remote locations, although by the 1990s, nearly all of these forgotten buses had been saved. Occasionally, however, exciting finds are made, often when sites are cleared and the vehicles are about to be scrapped. The British Bus Preservation Group, for example, located three E.C.W. bodied Leyland TD2s in a Norfolk yard in 1992 - they were new to Eastern Counties in 1933, and had survived well by being hidden under many trees. Similarly, the same year witnessed a West Midlands preservation group acquiring a 1930s Morris Dictator new to Birmingham City Transport that had had a house built around it !

The first point of contact with a vendor will usually be a telephone call, and you will probably only have a brief idea from an advertisement or other contact of what is for sale. If your information indicates what type of vehicle is on offer, do some homework before that initial call and satisfy yourself that the vehicle is the sort that you want to spend many hours and pound notes on. Some advanced investigations in your local public library (which often contain many books on buses and coaches) should enable you to obtain chassis and bodywork details, and the chance to study photographs and other notes.

Having made contact, endeavour to bypass "enthusiast" questions such as "who operated it first ?" and "what colour livery does it carry ?" which are of little relevance to the intending purchaser. Gaining answers to the following will be much more helpful when enquiring of vehicle sellers:

1. What is the condition of the vehicle chassis ?
2. Are the mechanics sound - when did it last run ?
3. What bodywork attention is required ?
4. Are tyres and batteries included in the price ?
5. Are the seats (and stairs) complete ?
6. Are there any modifications from standard ?
7. When does/did the M.O.T. expire ?
8. Has the vehicle been re-registered ?
9. Where is the vehicle situated ? (for viewing)
10. Is there a deadline on this sale ?

The question relating to a deadline on the vehicle sale is often overlooked by purchasers - and can lead to disappointment. Many vendors know that their vehicle may not sell, and will have made contingency plans to sell the bus for scrap value. If a date has been set, your work will be that much harder in sorting out the arrangements regarding your potential purchase, although a cash deposit is often quite successful in extending this period.

Your enquiry regarding the availability of seats and even a staircase for double-deckers is not as daft as it may at first seem. Seats may have been removed for a variety of reasons - the vehicle may have been a caravan, playbus or car transporter, for example, at some point in its history, and the seating and vehicle may never have become re-united. Staircases were often removed on double-deck vehicles used for driver training duties. If your intended purchase is lacking in either of these two important areas, then you will be subject to unavoidable costs which will probably stretch to at least several thousand pounds.

Similarly, the probing question concerning the vehicle registration should also be taken seriously. Any vehicle with a pre-1963 dateless registration without a year letter suffix has a number plate that is worth money. The original registration of the vehicle may already have been transferred elsewhere, or may be retained by the vendor after a sale has been agreed - any non-original registration will affect your vehicle's authenticity. It is worthwhile to note at this stage that a cherished registration is only valid if the vehicle is in possession of a current Vehicle Registration Document (V5) displaying that number: if it has been sitting in a field for several decades and can only produce an old green card type log book, then the registration has probably been withdrawn by DVLA at Swansea and may have been re-allocated to another vehicle. Further details on vehicle registrations can be found in the section The Law and Your Vehicle.

Having satisfied yourself that the vehicle is what you are looking for, any work needed is within your capacity and the vendor is genuine, the next essential step is to undertake a reasonably thorough examination. Never commit yourself before actually looking over a vehicle, regardless of its condition, and be prepared to travel the length and breadth of the country for this task. £20-30 spent visiting your selected bus at the other end of the country could save you several hundred pounds if it is a hopeless cause begging to be cut up for scrap.

What you inspect when you visit the vehicle depends on your level of technical knowledge and how dirty you are prepared to get, but as a rough guide, try and satisfy yourself as to the answers of the questions raised earlier. If your expertise is limited, try to take a knowledgeable person with you to give a second opinion. Assuming you are still willing to purchase after the inspection, the next stage is to agree a mutually acceptable price with the vendor - don't forget that whilst a good condition bus or coach will cost you more in initial outlay, this may be a better investment than a cheaper vehicle that requires a continual injection of funding during the course of restoration.

Many trade sources and dealers will charge VAT on the purchase price (this can make a big difference) and may also require that the batteries and/or tyres are bought separately. Private vendors rarely raise either of these potential stumbling blocks, and may even include some spare parts and manuals. Once a price has been agreed, probably the most painful part is handing over the money. If you are planning on removing the bus there and then, cash or a bankers order are likely to be the only acceptable currency: if you will have to make a second journey to collect, a personal cheque may have time to clear. Ensure that you receive a fully detailed receipt detailing exactly what has been sold and any conditions (eg no tyres), and if VAT has been charged obtain a VAT registration number. Also collect the vehicle registration document (complete the bottom portion and return this to the vendor), the MOT (if valid), keys (if applicable) and any relevant history of your vehicle that may be available (eg manuals, photographs etc).

## *Chapter 5*

## MOVING ELDERLY BUSES AND COACHES

DOING IT UNDER YOUR OWN STEAM .....

So by this stage you are the proud owner of an elderly Leyland PD2. The only problem is that it will probably be several hundred miles away from where you want it to be. The method of moving elderly passenger carrying vehicles is dictated by two factors - vehicle condition and law. The cheapest way of collecting your road-worthy bus is to drive it home, but there are legal constraints governing the suitability of this choice:

1.  Firstly, you must arrange adequate insurance cover as required by law. There are many brokers offering insurance for vehicles, and the wide variety of prices often equates to different conditions of acceptance or levels of cover, so check carefully. The Historic Commercial Vehicle Society also operates its own scheme for members: it is possible to arrange short period insurance (eg 1 day) if required.

2.  If your vehicle is to be driven, it must have a valid M.O.T. certificate. Without this, a vehicle cannot be driven unless it has been pre-booked into a Testing Station, and is actually travelling to this appointment. It has been known for preservationists to use this loophole to relocate there vehicle to where they want it, although if you are moving a bus from Inverness to an M.O.T. appointment in Brighton, this could be viewed as excessive and would be illegal.

3.  Unless travelling to a pre-booked M.O.T. test, your bus should also display a current tax disc. One possible alternative is to display trade plates, which are owned by motor dealers, bus companies and even some preservation organisations (eg the British Bus Preservation Group). Providing that a vehicle is insured and has an M.O.T., these plates allow vehicle movement between business sites and road testing without the need to display a tax disc. For further notes on the use of trade plates, see the chapter "The Law and Your Vehicle".

4. Even if your vehicle possesses a valid M.O.T. certificate and tax disc, ensure that the vehicle is currently legal before attempting to drive it. Check the condition and efficient operation of a number of areas before hand - tyres, brakes, steering, lights, windscreen wipers, etc, and carry out remedial repairs as necessary before commencing your journey.

If you decide to drive the vehicle, and can meet the above legal requirements, there are several other points which could help to ensure a trouble-free journey home. It is wise to take a support car with you to follow the new acquisition home. This should carry a large tool kit for unforeseen mechanical adjustments (or breakdowns), and could also act as a taxi to the nearest telephone if expert assistance has to be called upon. The route to be taken should be carefully planned in advance. Whilst preserved buses generally like motorways because of their constant speed, gentle bends and limited braking requirements, it is probably better to undertake your maiden voyage on A-roads for a number of reasons: breakdowns are more easily attended to on the side of an A-road than a motorway, it is safer to drive an unfamiliar vehicle on slower roads than on fast-moving motorways, and it is easier to stop for refreshments on non-motorway journeys - all the above are proven by experience ! If you have acquired a double-deck vehicle, be extremely cautious concerning overhead obstructions - particularly very immobile bridges, buildings and unlopped trees, all of which can severely damage your acquisition. Be aware of width and weight restrictions on your selected route, also.

## ..... OR USING SOMEONE ELSE'S STEAM

The chances are, however, that your bus will not be driveable and you will need to employ some professional assistance in order to encourage its movement. The condition of the vehicle you have just acquired will determine the most efficient means of transporting it, and there are three alternative methods.

If your relic has a sound chassis with a fully functioning rear axle, then the quickest, safest and most efficient method is to employ a recovery vehicle with hydraulic lifting equipment which will lift the front end clear of the ground: the truck will then steer as well as brake the vehicle on tow, and it is not necessary for anyone to travel inside the bus. If such a recovery truck is not available, you may have to use a vehicle which will tow by a fixed bar. The bar is rigidly connected to both vehicles, which allows the transfer of braking capacity, but the vehicle on tow must be steered behind the recovery truck. If the structure of your antique is not suited to running on its own wheels, then it will be necessary to hire a vehicle with a low-loader trailer to carry the bus on. A suitable means of loading the trailer will also be needed (eg winch, tractor).

A final thought, for the safety of both your vehicle and other road-users, ensure that a light board is installed at the rear for the duration of the tow. Such a board should display tail lights, stop lights, indicators and reflectors, as well as the registration plate of the towing vehicle. Many years ago, such an accessory was

*Former Devon General Leyland Atlantean 928 GTA prepares for a fixed bar tow whilst undergoing extensive restoration. This method of towing requires the bus to be steered, although the tow truck provides the total braking capacity.*

often overlooked, but with today's crowded road conditions (especially in heavy rain, fog or snow), it is essential to be as visible as possible.

Whatever method you choose, the following points should be carefully considered before making arrangements:

a) Try to choose a contractor or haulier with proven experience in the delicate art of collecting elderly buses and coaches (the British Bus Preservation Group maintains a list of companies with a good record of towing members' vehicles).

b) A company local to the ultimate destination for your vehicle is probably best as their reliability will be greater.

c) Try to arrange a reduced rate for off-peak towing (ie evenings or weekends) when the towing vehicle will probably otherwise be sitting idle.

d) Check relevant technical details well in advance:
   (i) Does the tow truck insurance cover the vehicle on tow ?
   (ii) Are there any height or weight restrictions en route ? (don't forget to include the tow truck statistics)
   (iii) If your vehicle is to have a suspended tow, will the rear axle half-shafts have to be removed ?
   (iv) If using a low-loader, will the well of the trailer be long enough to accommodate the bus or coach ?

(v) Are any auxiliary services necessary ? Don't overlook the potential requirements for a winch, crane or tractor for the extraction and loading of your vehicle.

e) If your journey involves the use of ferries, it will be necessary to arrange your crossings in advance. You will need exact weights of both the towing vehicle and its load, and also the end-to-end overall length. Check access to the ferries concerned, especially if boarding ramps with steep gradients have to be negotiated. Ferry charges invariably change throughout the year according to the holiday seasons - try to arrange a special rate for off-peak crossings.

f) Regardless of the means by which your bus or coach is to be moved, ensure that any loose body parts are secured by chains or rope. If the vehicle has not moved for some considerable period and if there is the possibility that panels or fitted parts might break off or be loosened and fall off by vibration, then it is a good idea to cover the entire vehicle with a net or tarpaulin - not only to prevent the loss of such parts, but also to protect other road-users !

No matter which method you choose, or the distance that has to be covered, it is essential that this very expensive exercise is planned well in advance. Hastily arranged collections involving buses that need several hours of loading using an ill-equipped recovery vehicle will undoubtedly result in unplanned expenses, and even then your vehicle may end up not being moved at all.

*Chapter 6*

# WHAT RESTORATION IS NEEDED ?

After your vehicle has finally been delivered to your chosen destination, take a good, long hard look at it as it stands forlornly in the corner of its barn. If you are one of the few fortunate individuals who has just purchased an immaculately restored Showbus, then the following sections will probably (and thankfully) not apply to you - so get polishing and excuse the rest of us for a few moments .....

There are many hundreds of different types of bus and coach that could be the subject of a preservation project, and a concise guide such as this could not possibly cover every aspect of the restoration of each individual marque. The following two chapters deal with a suggested methodical approach to the basic areas of mechanical and bodywork restoration, although it should be understood that relevant workshop manuals and technical expertise maybe required to complete a project satisfactorily and safely.

*Chapter 7*

# MECHANICAL AND ELECTRICAL THOUGHTS ...

In priority order, if your vehicle requires mechanical and electrical attention, then these are the areas that should receive your first thoughts as these are two aspects which are absolutely vital to the eventual running of your vehicle. Use your own good judgement, however, if your vehicle has large holes on the roof or in the side panels, or if windows are missing, attempt to make your vehicle weather-proof as a damage limitation exercise until the time comes for you to concentrate on the bodywork. An old tarpaulin or industrial plastic sheeting should be applied where needed using a waterproof adhesive tape. If your mechanical attentions eventually make your vehicle mobile, then this will make it easier to take your vehicle to specialist bodywork restorers, if necessary. Do not apply this rule in every case: if you are presented with one of those rare hot and sunny spells of weather, you may wish to take the opportunity to undertake some bodywork restoration yourself, as this type of attention relies on favourable weather for successful results.

*An unusual preservation candidate is this AEC Regal IV with Park Royal 1½ deck coachwork. New to British European Airways in 1953, only a handful of these distinctive coaches survive. This particular example, MLL 740, requires extensive bodywork restoration in this view.*

A guide such as this cannot attempt to cover all of the mechanical problems that you are likely to encounter on any one of several hundred vehicle types that may be nearly a century old. The following notes are a brief discussion of the various components and the attention they are likely to require, but you will also require access to an appropriate workshop manual, an experienced mechanic or other willing preservationists .......

## THE ENGINE

A good initial place to start is with your engine. Of course, if your relic does not possess one of these vital components, your first job is to locate and acquire one. A detailed examination of your engine and auxiliary components will already have given you some idea as to its general condition. Allow an experienced mechanic to examine your engine and associated components, and if parts are missing or the unit looks particularly fragile, then any necessary remedial work should be started. If, however, the unit looks as though it may function, carry out the following preliminary checks and then attempt to start it !

## PRE-IGNITION PRELIMINARY CHECKS

a) The fuel system preparations will be dictated by the vehicle fuel type. Petrol-engined vehicles require the same attention as per the average family car - the carburettor should receive adequate fuel by an efficiently operating fuel pump, spark plugs and contact points should be cleaned or replaced. Diesel-engined

*This exposed view of the engine bay and steering components of a Leyland PD2 shows many parts clearly. The wheel hub and brake pipes are foremost, with the suspension leaf springs just behind. The injector pump and pipes are visible under the exhaust manifolds, and the horn and sidelight can also be seen. Note the provision of a stout axle stand under the front cross-member whilst the wheel assembly receives attention*

counterparts are in many ways simpler to attend to, although injectors should be checked, cleaned or replaced to ensure efficient running. Again, a properly functioning injector pump to deliver fuel to the injectors is essential. In both cases, ensure that all fuel filters are flushed through with clean fuel, and that there is no stale diesel or petrol anywhere in the system. It may be necessary to bleed the fuel lines to release any trapped air bubbles which can exist in both types of system.

b) Checks should include the efficient, operation of the radiator and cooling system, and the proper circulation and retention of the correct quality of coolant. Flush the radiator through to check for leaks and blockages, and if a blockage is suspected, attempt to remove any debris using a long thin piece of wire. Ensure that the correct mixture of anti-freeze is present if you are working in the winter.

c) Unless you are certain of the vehicle's maintenance history, undertake a full oil and filter change, as the existing oil may have been there for decades. The condition of the old oil will give you a good indication as to the general engine condition, and will reveal the level of maintenance that it had previously received. Attend to lubricant leaks by replacing the offending gaskets, tightening bolts, etc, as they arise. Ensure that all used oil is disposed of correctly.

d) After noting the electrical precautions detailed below, connect a fully charged set of 12 or 24 volt batteries (care to ensure the correct type) ensuring good connections and the correct polarity. Visually check all accessible electrical leads and connections, and check and replace any faulty fuses with components of the correct rating.

e) Having carried out the above to your satisfaction, chock the wheels, apply the handbrake and ensure that the gear selector is residing in neutral. Activate the pre-heater on diesel engines, reset any fuel overload triggers, and prime the engine with fuel if a manual primer is fitted (an unprimed engine may never start). If your bus has a petrol engine, activate the choke if fitted.

f) Attempt to start the engine, either via the starter button, ignition key or starter handle as appropriate. If your engine starts and continues to run, wait a few moments for the unit to warm up and then listen to the sound of the engine. Any apparent uneven running can be attributed to temporary problems such as blocked injectors, an incorrect firing order, poor timing adjustment, poor fuel/air mix, or stuck valves. Once these matters have been rectified, continual poor running may indicate a worn engine that will have an area of more permanent damage.

## GENERAL FAULT DIAGNOSIS

g) If after several attempts you have had no success in achieving a running engine, you should be able to commence highlighting potentially faulty components. Avoid the temptation to use one of the readily available aerosols containing volatile fluids to start the engine: once so fed, they invariably become an essential requirement for the starting procedure on every occasion.

h) Assuming that your engine is not "seized" (ie has suffered permanent damage caused by its operation without adequate lubrication and cooling), if there is no activity whatsoever, the gear lever is in neutral and the battery is charged and has good electrical connections, suspect the electrical system and investigate accordingly. If your electrical system is of a negative earth format (see below), check that good earthing points exist to complete electrical circuits. Components such as solenoids and starter motors will probably not function properly if they have been unused for any length of time as damp may have caused rust to set in: starter motors and alternators that have suffered neglect will need professional re-conditioning.

i) If the engine readily turns over but fails to start, is there sufficient fresh fuel in the tank ? Old diesel can adopt a waxy consistency in fuel pipes, and old stale petrol can have an octane rating as low as 60. If fuel condition appears to be the problem, drain the tank and clean through the component pipes and pumps of the fuel system with new fuel. Some engines rely on a gravity feed system to deliver the fuel: the autovac, if fitted, should be checked and adjusted. When re-assembling, bleed the fuel pipes to remove any obstructive air bubbles.

j) Primed with sufficient fresh fuel, if your engine still refuses to co-operate then the electrical components are functioning but there may be a problem with the components of the fuel system. The electric fuel pump can be examined by disconnecting the outlet port(s), turning the engine over and watching for a stream of ejected fuel (take care as to where this fuel goes !). Any further investigations will need to concentrate on the condition of spark plugs and contact points in the distributor in petrol engines, as these are vital to fuel ignition. Check the ignition timing, as the spark plugs may be sparking at a point when there is no fuel in the cylinder. In diesel engines, remove the injectors and nozzles and have them professionally cleaned and calibrated, or replaced.

k) If your best attempts at starting your vehicle fail, fully carry out all the relevant checks as explained in the vehicle manual. If you still have no luck, seek an independent second opinion before resigning yourself to dismantling your engine for internal examination. Whatever repairs you are sure are necessary will be assisted by appropriate workshop manuals. Always ensure that any parts removed are adequately labelled and photographed if necessary to aid replacement, and that any old gaskets and seals are carefully removed and retained as they may be required as templates if new parts are not readily available.

## THE GEARBOX

Buses and coaches with well-maintained manual gearboxes will require little attention if they are regularly checked for lubricant levels. Clutches, however, will often require replacement, and when this is necessary, the gearbox will have to be removed - a fairly major task requiring several pairs of hands. When renewing clutches, ensure that all three parts of the assembly are renewed (plate, lining and thrust bearing), as only replacing the faulty component will be a false economy. The standard of driving employed can drastically change the life-span of a clutch, so a cautious approach could be financially beneficial in the long run. A driver who rides the clutch, ie rests his left foot on the clutch pedal whilst driving, will cause the rapid wear of clutch linings and the withdrawal bearings. Only in extreme cases will the gearbox either have to be replaced or rebuilt, and this is undoubtedly a job for the mechanical specialists in this field.

Vehicles equipped with compressed air systems often have gearboxes which require a supply of compressed air to ensure their efficient operation. A damaged or blocked air pipe can prevent a gearbox of this type functioning altogether. Take extreme care when investigating high pressure air lines, which can be quite lethal: ensure that the air system is empty before examining any component parts.

Automatic and semi-automatic gearboxes are extremely complicated mechanical units which will unavoidably require specialist servicing and repairs when problems arise.

## ELECTRICAL SYSTEM

The electrical problems encountered during restoration of old buses and coaches will probably take up most of your time and patience. Before any attempt to introduce current into the wiring looms of your vehicle, a visual inspection will tell you as to whether this is a wise decision. Old fabric covered wiring looms with frayed wires protruding from within are a sure way to ensure that your vehicle will catch fire - if your vehicle is like this, you should resign yourself to several days of rewiring your vehicle with new colour-coded wire, fuses and connectors to improve total safety (ensure you compile a comprehensive new wiring diagram as you go).

The electrical component that causes most problems is the battery. Buses and coaches will possess either a 12 volt battery or one or two units making a 24 volt battery. The vehicle battery should have clean terminals with tightly connected leads and it should be securely mounted in a dry, upright position. The specific gravity of the electrolyte (sulphuric acid and distilled water solution) should be checked using a hydrometer: the reading for each cell should be the same. If there is a requirement to replace any electrolyte, then a sulphuric acid solution is preferential to simply adding distilled water (which will cause dilution of the electrolyte), and a specialist should be consulted as the handling of any acid is particularly hazardous. Not all batteries are of this type - some are jelly-type sealed units that require no maintenance apart from charging when required. Designed for use on aircraft, the electrolyte consists of thick jelly which is enclosed in a sealed plastic container.

Your electrical system will be one of two types: double insulated or negative earth. Negative earth systems supply electrical components with power from the positive (+) side of the battery, whilst the negative (-) terminal has been connected to the chassis: hence any component in contact with the chassis or metallic bodywork will operate as the circuit has been completed. Beware - some vehicles possess a positive earth system ! Double insulated systems require each electrical component to be physically connected to both battery terminals - these systems require much more wiring than their negative earth counterparts in which the whole vehicle is effectively negative.

Under normal operating conditions, the battery will remain fully charged whilst the vehicle is running. Any current taken for the operation of the starter motor or any of the many electrical components that are fitted should be replaced by the action of the alternator (or generator) on modern vehicles. The alternator is driven by a fan belt(s) linked to the main shaft of the engine, and the revolution of magnets within the electric windings creates an alternating voltage, one half of each cycle being passed back to the battery: a second set of windings provides the alternate half cycle. Because the engine speed can vary greatly (as will the voltage produced) a controller or regulator may be installed to control the alternator output. Elderly vehicles may possess a dynamo, which provides an unregulated direct current to the battery. Alternators are more efficient than dynamos, and their reliability should ensure less electrical system charging problems; additionally the replacement of dynamos is becoming increasingly difficult.

There are a surprisingly large number of electrical components installed on an average passenger carrying vehicle, all of which a vehicle owner should be aware of. Obvious components are the external lighting, windscreen wipers, washers and the horn, but other less noticeable fittings such as interior lighting, dashboard instrumentation and warning lights, internal illumination and heater motors could all potentially demand your time and attention.

The correct functioning of the external lighting is an essential requirement for any road-going vehicle, and an area that often causes an M.O.T. test failure. At the front of the vehicle, two headlamps and two sidelamps must be fitted, and the two units of each set must be mounted at the same height. The headlights should be set so as to accurately direct a dipped beam and a main beam. A pair of rear lights, which must show red, should also be fitted at an equal height, and a stopping light(s) which illuminates upon depression of the foot brake pedal must also be fitted. The requirements for the stopping light will vary according to the age of your bus; some elderly examples do not require an example at all, some require one light on the offside, AEC Routemasters have one centrally mounted light, although most vehicles have a pair, one on each corner. All buses and coaches must be fitted with red reflectors to the rear. As regards direction indicators (trafficators), some form of lighting is necessary on all but very early vehicles. Unless amber semaphore units are installed, it will be necessary to have flashing trafficators installed at the front (which must be white or amber) and at the rear (which must be red or amber), and again they must be at an equal height. The lens on all lights should be complete and have no cracks, and there should be no corrosion in any of the units or the reflective surrounds.

During electrical restoration, it may prove useful to construct a test lamp from a 12/24v light bulb (depending on your system voltage) with two wires attached to the + and - bulb connections, each ending at the other extreme with a crocodile clip. This simple device will tell you if current is flowing at a particular point, can establish good earthing points in negative earth systems, and highlight faulty motors, relays, bulbs, etc. If electrical fuses keep blowing during the course of your work, then trace the cause of this problem rather than keep replacing the fuse: trace the illness and not the symptoms.

## THE PRINCIPLE OF COMPRESSED AIR COMPONENTS

Increasingly common in the latter half of this century has been the introduction of systems and components that are air operated. When the engine is running, an air compressor is activated by the crankshaft through a linkage arrangement. The air compressor forces air into a large reservoir, from which it can be drawn for a variety of uses. Some vehicles use compressed air to assist the hydraulic braking system, whilst others may have brakes which are totally operated by air. On more modern vehicles, the compressed air in the air reservoir is used to operate doors, windscreen wipers and even suspension systems. To prolong the life of the air system, emptying the reservoir at the end of the day will eliminate the risk of frost and ice damage that could be caused by moisture in the stored air. If there is an apparent loss of air pressure in a vehicle's system, the best way to locate any escape is to cover joins, pipe unions and any other area under suspicion with a concentrated soap solution, and watch for bubble formation. At all stages, be aware that a fully pressurised compressed air system can be very dangerous if there is a sudden loss of pressure for any reason.

## STOPPING, STRUCTURE AND STEERING

The whole strength or otherwise of your bus will depend on the condition of the vehicle chassis and other connected structural hardware. To examine and carry out work on the underside of your vehicle, it will be necessary to safely raise the vehicle to a good working height and then support it on solid axle stands or timber supports (alternatively use an inspection pit if one is available). When jacking a vehicle that can weigh in at over 10 tonnes, ensure that the jack being used has a capacity which exceeds the weight being raised. When jacking the rear of your vehicle, block the front wheels to prevent the vehicle from rolling forward (this precaution is necessary as the hand brake operates on the transmission axle). Remove the road wheels in turn, and then proceed inwards to examine brake assemblies.

Brake shoes and pads should be renewed if they are worn or fractured, and brake pipes and linkages in hydraulic systems investigated for signs of corrosion and leakages. Be extremely cautious when handling brake pads and shoes, as these may contain asbestos which is extremely hazardous to your health. When removing dust and other residue from the vicinity of a brake assembly, use a damp cloth to remove all traces, and then dispose of this safely. If brake assemblies seem reluctant to move, a few blows with a rubber mallet should ease the situation. The linings should be checked for wear (and replaced if necessary), and the brake drums should be checked for any marks or imperfections. If any such blemishes do exist, then they will require professional repair to ensure that future brake linings are not prematurely damaged.

Simple hydraulic and vacuum hydraulic systems reduce the amount of pressure that the driver needs to apply when activating the brakes. By means of pipes and pistons, a much increased pressure of brake fluid is transmitted to the brake assemblies. If a section of hydraulic pipe is found to be leaking, it will undoubtedly have to be replaced. Depending on the location of the fault, it will have to be decided as to whether the whole section should be replaced, or whether the offending zone can be cut out and only that section refitted using universal pipe joints. It may be required to dismantle and overhaul the brake cylinders on each wheel at this stage, as the internal seals which ensure an efficient exertion of pressure onto the brakes often perish with age. After re-fitting brake assemblies, it will be necessary to adjust them such that the brake pedal will require the correct amount of travel to activate the system, and it is essential to check that the brake pedal is effective on all of the wheels. Leaks in additional pipes to air pressure assisted braking systems are best detected by listening for the hiss of any escaping air when the brakes are activated (the vehicle will need to be running and a sufficient pressure allowed to build). Don't forget the hand brake system, which operates mechanically by a series of levers and wires on the rear brake shoes: here again adjustment may be necessary to ensure that the handbrake lever functions properly, and that the braking power is sufficient.

The tyres should be looked at carefully for any signs of damage. The tyre tread should be even across the entire width, and the depth should exceed the current minimum legal requirements. Tyres on the same axle should correspond not only in size, but also in construction type. Uneven wear may indicate distorted tyres or incorrect pressures, the wheel needs balancing (or it may be more seriously damaged), or that the tracking of the front wheels requires adjusting. If the tread on any tyre does not meet the current legal requirements, or if any steel or cord ply has worn through to the surface then the tyre should be replaced. Damage to the tyre side walls will have been caused by scuffing the tyres against kerbstones and other immobile obstacles: severe weakening of the side wall will require the tyre to be replaced.

Check that the tyre pressures are correct (this should be done at regular intervals), and that valves are not leaking. Vehicles with twin rear tyres may present access problems to the inner tyre, and a common valve or automatic adjustment mechanism should be installed to ensure equal pressure on both wheels. Care should be taken when fitting or removing bus tyres: they are very heavy objects that can cause serious injuries to the unwary. The wheel nuts should be tightened using the proper wheel-brace, which should be long enough to provide the great leverage necessary to tighten the wheel nuts to the recommended torque settings (acquire a torque wrench if necessary). When painting wheels, endeavour to avoid painting the wheel nuts, as this is not only cosmetically pleasing, but will prevent thick layers of paint building on a surface which has to fit the wheel brace. The security and serviceability of wheels and their tyres is one of the most important aspects of safety on your vehicle.

The chassis can now be examined for corrosion or damage. It may be necessary to remove several decades' contribution of oil, grease and dirt first, and a steam clean would be the most efficient way to reveal the chassis properly. Any chassis defects should be attended to at this stage, although this may require welding and plating expertise. Do not neglect other related components on the chassis such as the cross-members and mounting points. When your repairs are complete, it is essential to safeguard the underside by the application of a rust inhibiting coating. An aluminium paint coating (which will show oil leaks) is compulsory for vehicles which are to undergo a PCV examination, and on any vehicle, such a silver coating always looks better than simply leaving the underside coated with a dull, rust inhibitor.

Whilst your vehicle is still aloft, this presents the preservationist with a good opportunity to attend to other usually inaccessible systems such as the exhaust and steering assemblies. It can be an impossible task whilst the vehicle is resting on its wheels to check the efficient functioning and correct lubrication of the steering box and related components, (such as track rod ends, wheel bearings and ball joints) or to check the secure mounting and condition of a section of exhaust, so this chance to examine at leisure should be taken. You should also be able to access suspension components at this stage, and identify and replace leaking and corroded shock absorbers, cracked or fractured leaf springs and damaged king pins and anchorage bolts. Having satisfied yourself that all of the components of the under-side are functioning efficiently and that the chassis structure is sound and protected from future corrosion, replace the wheels and lower the vehicle.

## Chapter 8

## BODYWORK - RESTORATION VS REPLACEMENT

For most individuals, the ownership of a historic bus or coach is a long-term commitment that will witness the vehicle being kept by the same owner for many years. It is on this understanding that any repairs that are carried out to the bodywork of your vehicle should be effected so as to be as permanent as possible, so that once done, they can be forgotten about for up to a decade or so.

BODYWORK

Before starting any bodywork repairs, step back for a moment and take a quantitative look at the amount of work to be undertaken. Any areas of rust should be removed by a wire brush, to reveal the extent of underlying damage caused by possibly years of water penetration. Plan a course of action on two criteria, firstly select those tasks that you feel able to complete yourself and list separately those where expert assistance is required, secondly allocate priorities to both lists so as to undertake urgent and damage limitation work first, with minor dents and scratches being a last minute finishing touch. It will be prudent to be methodical when approaching bodywork repairs - start at the front and work your way round in one direction. And for those that have got a Bristol Lodekka standing in front of you - wouldn't a small single-decker have been an easier choice ?

Up until quite recently, many buses and coaches in particular were constructed to a large extent with wooden frames forming part (or sometimes all) of the bodywork structure. By looking along the waistrail of a wooden-framed bus, the beading under the windows should be straight. If it is not, it would be prudent to remove any surface panels or other internal coverings to inspect these potentially rotten (and hence structurally dangerous) areas with a view to their urgent renewal. When removing old wooden sections, it is always wise to try and keep the original sections for patterns, labelling each as they are extracted - although rotten sections will often come away with the body panels. Don't forget that rotten, water-sodden wood will probably have been distorted and had its original dimensions changed somewhat - be cautious of the originality of all wood used for patterns ! When fabricating new wooden parts, ensure that seasoned wood is used (unseasoned wood will distort with time), and that a liberal application of preservative is applied before mounting.

Metal frameworks tend to last for much longer periods than their wooden counterparts without requiring attention. For a long-term restoration, however, these too should be carefully examined for signs of corrosion (particularly at structural joints) and appropriate renovation work carried out. The penetration of many years worth of rainfall will find parts of the framework which you could never have imagined existed! A further area of weakness to consider is that of the electrolytic corrosion caused where aluminium and steel components join: with the help of rain water and road salt, the aluminium very quickly turns to a powder and will require complete replacement. Whilst such frameworks are totally fabricated from metal, they may well possess wooden mounting blocks upon which panels and trim can be affixed. These components often require renewal.

In all areas where existing metalwork that has suffered from some degree of corrosion is to remain, then careful preparation of affected regions is necessary. Through cleaning by a wire brush and emery cloth will reveal clean metal under the rust, which should then be promptly treated with a rust inhibitor to prevent re-occurrences. Many rust inhibitors will actively turn any remaining traces of rust into another stable metal oxide.

Two potential areas of weakness that are often overlooked are those at either end of the vehicle which are not directly supported by the chassis. Over-hanging rear platforms and protruding drivers' cabs may be supported by sections of framework mounted further back on the chassis, and these exposed sections should demand your careful examination to identify if any major structural corrosion or fatigue has set in.

Care should also be taken if any of the roof framework has been identified as requiring replacement as the structure of buses and coaches relies upon these roof members for an essential part of the overall rigidity of the vehicle. These sections of roof should be carefully removed one panel at a time, so as not to significantly reduce the upper body strength. Having replaced the offending wooden or metal beams, it will be prudent to use a waterproof sealant when remounting roof panels and any associated beading, as this is one area where water penetration is most likely to occur.

If complete panel replacement is viewed as necessary, either due to accident damage or severe corrosion, then a decision will have to be made as to the viability of this based on several factors. The overall size of the panel concerned will need to be evaluated - it may well be the full length of your vehicle which will cause financial problems as well as many cross words when trying to re-mount the new part ! The structural position of the panel should be carefully considered, as some components (such as the front bulkhead and roof domes) will need to be fabricated with particular attention to their strength. The complexity of the panel should also be carefully examined - it may contain window ledges, wheel arch channels, rain gutters, or ventilation inlets, all of which will have to be re-created from a new piece of metal. The choice of material (mild steel, galvanised steel, aluminium or even fibreglass) will be a matter of choice, based on availability, panel size, cost and the existing vehicle panels. One cheap option may be to purchase second-hand panels that are larger than your requirements, and cut them down to size as necessary. This approach can be a particularly useful solution to the problems of making wheel-arch panels, where it can be extremely difficult to maintain circular regularity. Current practice amongst some preservationists is to replace original steel panels with lighter and longer-lasting aluminium equivalents, although care should be taken to avoid compromising the strength of steel panels for the sake of a weight saving.

To aid the bodywork restoration which is executed from inside the vehicle, it is helpful to have removed all of the interior fixtures and fittings. This will not only allow you more room in which to work, but also permit the removal of side panels and flooring to expose any underlying damaged areas: at this stage any area of damaged flooring should be replaced. The front roof dome of double-deckers is particularly susceptible to damage from over-hanging trees (and occasionally buildings), and due to its complexity, any indentations are best hammered out from the inside, with any remaining imperfections being dealt with by body filler applied externally. The efficient and safe operation of any entrance and exit doors is a time-consuming area where it may be necessary to replace worn out hinges and guidance rails to ensure satisfactory safe operation. doors are usually very heavy and cumbersome, requiring several pairs of hands, and their movement can be encouraged by the application of a lithium-based grease to the moving parts.

For non-structural repairs on bus bodywork, many well known products and techniques that are readily applied to cars and other small vehicles can be used. The use of fibreglass, which is a strong and durable yet lightweight material, will often be necessary, whether to bridge holes or create patterns and moulds of existing body parts. Fibreglass is ready available in kit forms, and with careful mixing of resin and hardener before applying to fibreglass matting, a permanent repair can easily be affected (provided that thorough preparation of the surrounding areas has already been carried out). The selection of body fillers and other similar products should be undertaken cautiously - their uses are often fairly restricted on large, rattly buses and coaches. Most brand-name fillers are ideal for filling small holes and dents, but any larger applications may cause some problems. Traditionally, body filler expanded and contracted at different rates to the vehicle bodywork with rises and falls in temperature, causing unsightly cracks. Similarly, their rigid setting state was readily dislodged by the constant vibration of our beloved buses and coaches. Some modern products now claim to be flexible, which should remove these aforementioned problems: only your experimentation will reveal the brands that are best suited to different applications. When using body fillers and fibreglass which require sanding to create a smooth finish, ensure that a face mask is worn at all times to prevent the inhalation of the resulting particles. Such work is best carried out in a well ventilated area.

## VEHICLE GLAZING

Special care should be taken when renewing window panels, or when generally handling the glazing of your vehicle. Many windows will be large, bulky and consequently heavy, and mistakes often lead to costly breakages. If body glass has to be removed, you are advised to consult a local automotive glass specialist as to the safest and most efficient way to undertake this often difficult task. Roof cants (both the glass and plastic varieties) are extremely difficult to remove and replace as their pre-formed curvature makes them very rigid with little or no flexibility. Some coaches with full-drop side windows will require the removal of internal side facia panels in order that the operating mechanism can be accessed. Owners of older vehicles will usually find the need to replace old and brittle window rubbers, and a new supply of the same specification should be made available when fitting new glass or refitting the existing glazing. The same caution should be given to the glass fronts of destination displays and rear number plates.

## TRIM, FIXTURES & FITTINGS

As regards the remainder of your bodywork, for example the interior trim, seating fitting and spacing, luggage racks, bell buttons, etc then the number of these tasks will vary enormously from vehicle to vehicle. If you have components that require repair or renewal, you may experience problems finding suppliers of trim or material that can exactly match the existing vehicle specification, which may have become significantly faded over the years. Fortunately, there are an increasing number of specialist sources that can manufacture replacement parts or alternatives for many bodywork parts - from bumpers to interior lights shades and seat headrest covers to period first aid kits: your choice will be limited only by the amount of time you want to spend on the telephone - and your wallet.

A visit to the premises of the local breaker will prove useful for the acquisition of spare parts from vehicles undergoing dismantling, whilst the hundreds of auto-jumbles and bus rallies up and down the country each year often have stalls with second hand bus and coach spares available. You should endeavour to retain the overall authenticity of your vehicle throughout this stage - refrain from installing any components which are visibly obvious as products of the 1990s.

Some other components that you may have forgotten about also come under the heading of fixtures and fittings. If your bus is to be fitted with destination blinds you will need to acquire a set containing the correct information. Similarly, vehicles of decades past often displayed fare charts and route information cards internally, and these too will have to be located. Such specific items are likely to be extremely rare, and may only survive in the archives of specialist collectors. Some preservationists have resigned themselves to creating copies.

## PAINTWORK

Before starting the expensive and time-consuming procedure of painting your vehicle, ensure that all other restoration to the bodywork has been fully completed,

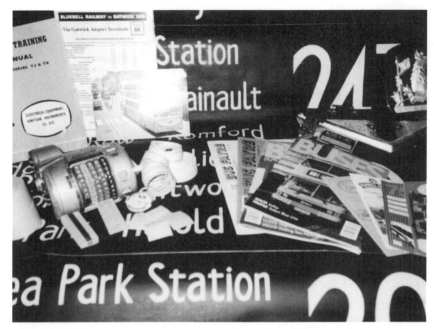

*Just some of the many items that you may require to complete an authentic restoration: destination blinds, maintenance manuals, ticket machines, staff badges, timetables, route cards, insignia and enthusiast magazines - to name but a few!*

as there is little point in spending many hours applying expensive paint to body panels that will have to be removed or replaced in the near future. The method of applying a livery to your bus and coach is another decision which has to be made by the vehicle restorer - should it be hand painted by brush or spray applied ? But first things first, the area to be painted will have to be prepared thoroughly to achieve a satisfactory result.

Ideally, all existing paint will be totally removed so that the new paint will have a sound base. Your vehicle may have up to a dozen coats of old paint still resident, and there are two ways to remove the liveries of decades past. The most common method is the application of a coat of paint stripper or remover, and there are many products on the market that perform this task. After a short period, the paint is loosened and blisters, making it a comparatively easy task to remove unwanted paint with a stripping tool. This approach may require several applications in order to remove a particularly thick build-up, and care should be exercised such that only the areas that require stripping are so treated. The cost of such fluids may prevent their use in quantity, for example if treating the entire body of a double-deck vehicle. An alternative approach favoured by a few individuals is the use of a hot air gun (either electric or butane gas) to burn old paint off. Care must be exercised to avoid excessive heating which may cause panels to expand, and only short localised bursts of heat should be used. This method should not be used near areas of wooden trim and framework, and near any body glass and window rubbers - for obvious reasons. Any body filler that is hiding under old paint will be damaged by

*GXX 785 is an AEC Matador Recovery Unit which has been restored in the livery of its last owner, Southern Vectis. It remains fully operational, however, and has assisted many a troubled preserved bus!*

the use of a heat gun. Whatever method is chosen, wear a breathing mask that will protect you from smoke and dust particles, and use a well ventilated area for this task.

Once all of the body panels have been cleared back to an unpainted state, any exposed rust should be dealt with and small dents and imperfections should be filled and sanded to achieve a totally flat surface for painting. The surrounding areas that are not to be painted should be masked using old newspapers and adhesive tape, and finally those areas left exposed for painting should be dusted using a clean dry cloth to remove any dust.

Hand painting is probably the cheapest of the two options, as it requires no specialist equipment. Several undercoats should be applied upon those areas already prepared for painting, and a light sanding between each coat will remove any blemishes or runs. In order to keep airborne dust particles to minimum, it is a good idea to sprinkle water on the ground around and under the bus. Ensure that the colour of the undercoat is compatible with the planned top coat. The top coat should also be applied in two or three coats, and all but the very last coat should be sanded as before to guarantee a smooth finish. When complete, it is a common practice to apply a coat of clear varnish to preserve the colours and exhibit a glossy finish to the livery.

Spray painting will be quicker and use less paint, but it is an expensive process which will require specialist paint spraying equipment. There will be no need to sand in between each application of undercoat or top coat, as the spraying technique should leave a perfect finish. A recent development utilised by some preservationists is the application of a spray livery, and then a final hand painted top coat to retain an authentic finish.

Be aware that certain types of different paints will react with each other to give a shoddy appearance: applying lead-based enamels over cellulose-based products, for example, will provide a good pattern for crazy paving your patio ! Matching new paintwork to existing livery (which may be faded) is another area that will provide you with hours of amusement. It is often necessary to use a colour restoring compound to bring back the original livery colours of areas you are trying to match.

Only remove the original fleet names, logos or lettering from a vehicle if you are sure that replacement decals are available. There are a number of specialist companies which can re-create such complex artwork providing that detailed photographs and measurements are made available. Some fleet names are so rare that preservationists have been forced to spend many hours painting around the originals so that they may remain.

## SUMMARY

All bodywork restoration, from a complete rebuild right down to the replacement of interior trim, requires careful thought and preparation to ensure a successful end result. Always be sure that you can complete any tasks that you propose undertaking, and that all the materials and parts required are available before you commence such work. When using chemicals or fluids that carry health warnings, read these carefully and take all reasonable precautions as advised. Where necessary, engage the skills and tools of experts to ensure that your bodywork is restored to a standard that will last for many years.

## Chapter 9

## AUTHENTICITY - IS IT PRACTICAL ?

The object of owning an elderly passenger carrying vehicle to most preservationists is to present an image which accurately reflects the original condition of the bus or coach in question. Retaining the authenticity of your pride and joy will require a little more attention (and finance) if you are to be successful in returning it to "as delivered" condition. The following points highlight some advantages and disadvantages which you may experience when striving to recreate that authentic finish.

The original mechanical units may be unserviceable and in need of attention, and you may be considering replacing them with more modern equivalents. Whilst

*Hastings Trolleybus 3 (DY4965), a Dodson bodied Guy BTX Trolleybus built in 1928, is powered by a Commer petrol engine which was fitted in the 1960's. This non-original source of motion has allowed the continual rallying and public use of this trolley, long after the overhead wiring had disappeared. It is seen here at the Eastbourne Buses' 90th Anniversary celebrations in July 1993, and after operating the free bus service fully laden for much of the day!*

it would be best to retain the original engine and gearbox in terms of the vehicle's value, consider the financial advantages of installing and running a modern diesel unit over rebuilding a tired petrol engine. If you intend travelling extensively, an efficient diesel that may save you many pounds in fuel over the original engine may convince you that this slight deviation from the original is perfectly acceptable. The infamous hastings Dodson-bodied Guy Trolleybus DY 4965 dating from 1928 represents another school of thought: this particular vehicle had its electrical trolley motors replaced with a Commer petrol engine to enable it to run on its own power long after the overhead electric cable network had disappeared - it still attends rallies today.

The bodywork in its original form will ideally be to the specification that was delivered when new. Preservationists are generally very meticulous over the removal of non-original body parts, whether that means the restoration of covered staircases that were exposed when new, or the refitting of original metal panels that have long since been replaced by modern plastic or fibreglass counter-parts. It will be necessary to hunt for original photographs of your vehicle in order to ascertain whether the correct bodywork format is still carried. In extremely unusual cases, however, an experimental conversion or unorthodox adaptation may warrant the preservation of the resulting "hybrid". A good examples of this is the Northern General Tynesider (MCN 30K), which was originally a 1950s Leyland Titan adapted to forward entrance, one-man-operation format with the addition of an AEC Routemaster bonnet. This unique, strange-looking vehicle was rescued from an uncertain fate by the British Bus Preservation Group in 1992, and is now owned and under restoration by Blue Triangle of Bootle.

The seating in your vehicle may not be the original items installed when new, or they may be installed in a non-standard format. Seats may be missing or damaged, or you may have more than a dozen different moquettes amongst the full set. Your available finances will dictate whether you will be able to purchase an authentic set, re-cover the offending newcomers, or simply tolerate the existing miscellany. It is worth considering the size of this task before undertaking to restore seating authenticity in one go - the London Transport Leyland-engined RTL-class, for example, has 112 different seat cushions with no less than 12 different sizes !

The authenticity of your vehicle's electrical system and components may have to be sacrificed in the interests of safety. As mentioned previously, antiquated fabric-covered wiring looms should be replaced with new materials to prevent the risk of fire. For your own safety, you may wish to consider increasing the power of the bulbs in your headlights to assist any night driving: at the other end, your rear lights should be provide sufficient illuminance to be seen from a significant distance by following drivers. Many early vehicles were equipped with small, low power rear light units which were mounted behind thick lenses - the low intensity red light that was visible has contributed to many rear end collisions over the years.

The paintwork of your vehicle should ideally reflect the original owner or operator of the bus, and should be applied in the same way as it would have been when new. Certain municipal fleets still apply liveries by hand as they have always

*Authenticity is often sacrificed to portray an alternative side of a vehicle's history. Former London Transport AEC Routemaster ALD 993B has retained its later livery, acquired after purchase by Southampton Citybus.*

done, whereas other fleets migrated to spray painting at a very early stage. If your finances allow, you should attempt to locate the precise details of how the livery for your coach would have been applied, and if possible, recreate this exact method. Of course your livery does not have to be that of the original operator: there are an increasing number of rally entrants who have chosen to depict the vehicle in the livery of a successor fleet. Many former London Transport AEC Routemasters are currently entering preservation in the colours of their most recent non-London owners - eg Southampton Transport Southend Transport and Stagecoach subsidiaries.

Finishing touches can either greatly contribute to or completely detract from the overall level of authenticity. The most obvious error made by several preservationists in recent years has been the fitting of modern reflective number plates, where these were never previously carried. The fleet names and emblems carried should correspond as closely as possible to the original format - ensure that legal lettering, etc is completed in a period script. Try to locate details of any odd fittings that are unique to your type that may have been neglected: for example many Bristol Lodekkas started life with white window rubbers, most having since been fitted with conventional black replacements, and some vehicles were fitted with white steering wheels to indicate a vehicle width of 8' when this width was first authorised.

And what of modern technology ? Whilst many coaches from the mid-1950s onwards may have been equipped with a wireless for the benefit of the passengers, it is sad to note that some vehicles have been preserved with a more modern sound

*The bus rally of the 1990s presents the opportunity to view all kinds of bus and coaches. New or old, bus or coach, single or double deck, half-cab or full-front : all are visible in this line-up at the Romney, Hythe and Dymchurch Railway gathering in Kent in June 1993.*

*To celebrate their 90th anniversary in 1993, Eastbourne buses re-acquired this 1950 AEC Regal III from a private owner. Seen at the 1991 Cobham bus gathering, this East Lancs bodied bus has been restored to such a high standard by its new (and original) owner that it can be used in service.*

system ! If these must be fitted to relieve the engine noise of long journeys, then should they not be located out of sight or behind a cover ? Not all modern technology should be condemned, however. A fully working tachograph will be an essential accessory if your vehicle is to work for its living, although it may be advisable to house this unauthentic necessity in the vehicle dashboard (if practical) to make it a little less conspicuous.

So it can be seen that the level of authenticity amongst a row of vehicles on a rally field will vary greatly according to the individual preferences and restoration skills of the vehicle owners. Whilst a vehicle's proximity to its original condition may determine the outcome of a judged event, it is always pleasing to see those vehicles that can display an indication of their interesting subsequent histories.

# Chapter 10

## THE LAW AND YOUR VEHICLE

DRIVING LICENCES

It is essential that you hold a driving licence that allows you to drive your bus and coach legally. It is generally known that buses and coaches are long and wide vehicles that require special driving skills, and all professional drivers have to pass a PCV (Passenger Carrying Vehicle) Driving Test in order that they may drive vehicles in Category D for hire or reward. The driving licence system has been changed many times in the past few years in order to bring the United Kingdom into line with the European Community practice, and further changes are imminent. Full details of the current (1995) categories of licence which apply to buses and coaches are as follows (minimum driving age of 21 years applies):

Class D1    (formerly Group A) - small passenger carrying vehicles between 9 and 16 passenger seats not used for hire or reward.

Class D     (limited to 16 passenger seats) (new category) - as for class D1, but driving permitted for hire or reward purposes.

Class D     (not more than 5.5 metres long) (old PSV class 4) - more than 8 passenger seats, but vehicle length no more than 5.5 m.

Class D     (old PSV class 3) - large passenger carrying vehicles with more than 8 passenger seats regardless of length.

Class D&E (old PSV class 1 or 2) - articulated buses and buses towing trailers of more than 750 kg.

However, a number of vehicles can be driven without Category D entitlement, and these are as follows:

Small passenger carrying vehicles (9-16 passenger seats). Where the driver holds D1 entitlement which has been granted because an old Group A was in existence, small buses and coaches with between 9 and 16 seats can be driven, although this must not be for hire or reward. See the notes below, however, for restrictions dictated by the Second E.C. Directive (1996).

Historic Buses and Coaches. Any vehicle more than 30 years old from date of registration (a rolling date) can be driven by a person holding a conventional car licence providing it carries no more than 8 passengers and is not being used for hire or reward purposes. See the notes below, however, for restrictions dictated by the Second E.C. Directive (1996).

LGV Licence Holders. Holders of a Large Goods Vehicle (LGV) licence can drive any size vehicle of any age providing that no more than 8 passengers are carried and it is not being used for hire or reward purposes.

DVLA leaflet D200 contains full current details with respect to licensing, and should be studied in detail for concise regulations. It is worth noting that seating capacity plays an important part in the suitability of vehicles which are under 30 years old and which are therefore not deemed to be historic. It is not sufficient to purely remove the seats from a vehicle whose capacity exceeds 16 passenger seats in order that a D1 entitlement may be used, as the empty space remaining is still able to carry passengers, albeit standees. The empty space must be used up in other ways (installation of tables, etc), although care must be taken not to caravanise the interior, as this will invalidate most preserved policies of many insurance companies who are only interested in genuine buses and coaches. You could, however, then insure the vehicle as a caravan .....

A second EC Directive is due to be introduced on 1st July, 1996. This change will only affect those drivers who pass their car driving test (Category B entitlement) after this date - they will then only be permitted to drive vehicles with up to 9 seats including the driver's. In order that a vehicle of 9 to 16 seats may be driven (current Category D1), a restricted PCV test will have to be taken to gain the appropriate class. Larger vehicle drivers, as now, will continue to require P.C.V. testing. In addition, new drivers from the above date will no longer be entitled to drive historic vehicles under the 30 year ruling. This change to these driving entitlements will only affect those drivers who gain their car driving licence after this date: existing drivers who currently use either a D1 entitlement or the 30 year ruling will not be affected.

## VEHICLE REGISTRATION AND REGISTRATION MARKS

When you pay for your vehicle, you should expect to receive from the vendor the Vehicle Registration Document (V5). The top half of this gives details of the vehicle and its ownership, and you should amend the ownership details to your own and return this document to DVLA at Swansea as soon as possible so that a new V5 can be prepared in your name. The bottom half of the document is retained by the vendor - this is a notification of sale which he is obliged to send to DVLA separately. If no V5 is available, it is still possible to acquire one from DVLA by notifying them of your acquisition of the vehicle, but be wary of the vendor and satisfy yourself that he is legitimately entitled to sell the vehicle to you.

If only an old green Registration Book (VE 60) is available, then the vehicle has not changed hands since the DVLA records were computerised in 1984, and you will have to apply for a new V5 document. If the vehicle had a non-suffix registration, the DVLA will probably have assumed this to be no longer required and you will have to re-apply for the original number. There is a chance that it may have been transferred elsewhere - you may end up with another registration mark altogether. For further details, see the following notes on vehicle registrations.

Within the last decade or so, registrations that show no date identity (by way of a year letter) have become increasingly sought after and have realised a certain value. Many old buses and coaches have become the unwilling donors of their original registrations and have received new numbers with an A or B year identification suffix in exchange. The same new identity also affected elderly vehicles that were not registered on the DVLA computer by the end of 1984 - their original number had been assumed redundant, and a new set of A suffix registrations were issued. If your vehicle does not possess its rightful registration, there are a number of things you can do.

Firstly, you can now register a vehicle on the DVLA computer under its original number, provided you have reasonable evidence of what that number is (old log book, MOTs, tax discs, etc) which must additionally be authenticated by a classic vehicle organisation recognised for this purpose by DVLA. If you are successful in regaining the registration, it becomes non-transferable and cannot be changed again. The necessary forms for this application are available from all Local Vehicle Licensing Offices (LVLOs). The same procedure applies to those vehicles that had received a dateless SU or SV-series number (from unused Scottish registration blocks) in exchange for their original registrations before 1991 - apply to a LVLO in the same way as detailed above.

If you have purchased a bus or coach with a non-original registration, there is the possibility that the original number is now correctly displayed on another vehicle. Unless it is one of the few vehicles first registered in 1963 that received an A-suffix when new, any pre-1964 bus with such a mark has become a number donor at some time in its history. If, however, it was first registered before 31st December 1962, you can now apply to your nearest LVLO for a free period registration, which when granted becomes non-transferable.

Two exceptions to the above should be noted. Vehicles in possession of a Q-prefix registration have a non-transferable number: at some point these vehicles have been identified as having an unknown age, and the Q indicates this uncertainty. Former military vehicles lose their Ministry of Defence registrations when sold out of service - for example the author's Willowbrook-bodied Bedford J2SZ2 registration UVP 94S was new in 1969 to the Royal Navy as 12 RN 77, it was withdrawn from service in December 1976, and by the time it reached the Birmingham Police it had received an S-suffix plate which equates to the date it was sold, April 1978. Vehicles that are brought in from overseas are treated in a similar way if their age is known, else a Q-plate is allocated.

## INSURANCE

As with all road vehicles, preserved road passenger transport vehicles are required to be insured against third party risks as a minimum requirement - it is a serious offense to drive a vehicle with no effective insurance. Drivers of large buses and coaches must be over 21 years of age, although it is extremely difficult to gain insurance for a double-deck vehicle if you are under 25. There are many different policies available, but each will offer different levels of cover, damage excess payments, usage restrictions and passenger carrying limits, so be prepared to shop around to locate the policy that is right for you. Several insurance companies offer policies specifically geared to the requirements of bus preservationists, and certain societies (e.g. Historic Commercial Vehicle Society) have their own schemes with specialist insurance brokers which members are encouraged to partake in. Such specialist schemes, however, will often only accept historic vehicles built before a certain date (eg 1970), and owners of more modern buses and coaches will find the choice of available policies restricted as a result.

If you intend taking your vehicle to rallies and events, most organisers will require details of your insurance policy to ensure that it is in order, and you will usually have to sign an indemnity to guarantee that the policy in force adequately covers public liability and rally usage. Before you sign such a declaration, check your insurance certificate carefully.

## M.O.T. TESTING AND TAXATION

The type of M.O.T. (Ministry of Transport) test that your vehicle will be required to pass will depend on its size and the proposed duties it will perform. A full PCV (Passenger Carrying Vehicle) will require a Class VI test in order that it may be used to carry fare-paying passengers, and this will be taken at the nearest specified Department of Transport testing station. The requirements for a full Class VI test are more exacting than those detailed below for Class IV and Class V tests, and as many preservationists will not be testing their vehicle to Class VI, these requirements are not explained here. Refer to the nearest Department of Transport Class VI testing station for a full list of current requirements. Preserved vehicles (along with community buses and education authority vehicles) require a simpler Class V test, which will be undertaken at the same place as for a Class VI test. If your vehicle has between 9 and 12 seats, it will be eligible for a Class IV test at your local testing station (providing they are equipped to perform such an examination), and vehicles with less than eight seats undertake the standard car M.O.T. test.

The basic items under examination are as follows:

- Lighting Equipment (condition and operation of all external lights and reflectors, aim of headlights)

- Steering and suspension (steering control and mechanism, power steering, transmission shafts, wheel bearings, front and rear suspension, shock absorbers)
- Braking System (condition of service and parking brake systems, performance of service and parking brakes)
- tyres and wheels (tyre type and load speed ratings, condition and tread depth of road wheels)
- Condition (chassis and mechanical components free of cracks, bodywork free of protruding jagged edges)
- General (windscreen wipers, windscreen washers, horn, condition and security of exhaust system and fuel system)

In recent years, these have been increased to include the following additional items:

- Seat Belts (mounting, condition and operation if fitted)
- exhaust Emissions (both diesel and petrol engines)
- Windscreen (free of cracks, driver's view of the road)
- Registration Plates (character type and spacing, illumination)
- Auxiliary lighting (eg fog lights, reversing lights)
- Mirrors (provision, mounting and condition)
- Door Locks (condition, security of operation)

Amongst the new requirements mentioned above are a number of items that may not be fitted to your vehicle. The general view on such items is that if they exist, then they must function properly. Hence if you do not possess front fog lights there is no problem, but if they are fitted but do not work, then that is a cause of failure. Similarly, if your bus has an opening wind-screen, then windscreen wipers and washers are not compulsory, but if they have been fitted they must be fully operational. An additional feature of the test for buses and coaches is the material of which the windows are fabricated. Any body glass components that have been replaced by plastic windows may be a cause of failure on the M.O.T. test.

As 1994 drew to a close, there was an ongoing problem regarding the exhaust emissions of diesel engines. These tests were introduced at the start of 1993, and were temporarily withdrawn after only six weeks due to serious problems encountered when testing emissions of engines under full throttle under no load (often resulting in consequential engine damage). At the present time, some testing stations have re-introduced diesel testing whilst the engine is idling, whereas other stations still do not carry out this test. Enquire of your nearest testing station to satisfy yourself of the current testing requirements with regard to diesel engine emissions.

The above is a rough guide of the main areas that will be inspected: for fuller details, contact the testing station that will be carrying out your test. If any items warrant failure, a detailed failure sheet (VT30) will be supplied showing the areas that need rectification before a re-test is carried out. If the vehicle passes, then a Test Certificate (VT20) will be issued which lasts for twelve calendar months (or up to 13 months if the vehicle is tested not more than one month before the expiry of an exiting M.O.T. certificate). Make a note of the expiry date, as no reminders will be sent when it expires.

Armed with an M.O.T. certificate, a certificate of insurance (not the policy, schedule or a photocopy) and your Vehicle Registration Document V5 (if the vehicle does not currently have a tax disc that has just expired), a trip to your local main post office will bring you a P.L.G. (Private / Light Goods) tax disc - the same class as cars and light vans - if that is sufficient for your intended use of the vehicle. If your Registration Document V5 displays some other taxation class such as Hackney which you want modifying, this will have to be submitted to DVLA for modification to P.L.G. status. The cost of the PLG tax disc rises steadily in every Budget, although in early-1995 it cost £74.25 for six months or £135.00 for one year.

## THE USE OF TRADE LICENCES (TRADE PLATES)

If you are the registered owner of trade licences or have legitimate access to a set, the following notes should be read as a brief guide as to the issue of trade licences, their permitted uses, related offenses and other general notes. For full details, reference should be made to DVLA form VTL301/1.

The Department of Transport decides as to whether to grant an individual trade plates. The applicant should either be a vehicle trader (generally speaking manufacturers or repairers of, or dealers in mechanically propelled vehicles) or a vehicle tester (generally speaking an individual other than a vehicle trader who regularly tests vehicles belonging to others as a business). A vehicle trader or tester may only use trade licences on vehicles which are not owned by him but only temporarily in his possession, and permitted uses may include the following: tests or trials of vehicles after construction, modification or repair; return journeys to public weigh bridges or an authorised inspection appointment; tests or trials for a prospective purchaser or for the Press; movement of vehicles between traders' premises; proceeding to and from places of test or places of breaking or dismantling. For this last usage, the vehicle concerned must have a valid MOT, otherwise it must be towed to its ultimate destination. Vehicles travelling under trade plates are exempt from MOT requirements only if they are to be submitted for test upon completion of repairs.

A few of the offences which relate to trade licences are as follows: making false declarations to gain trade licences, to use trade licences on a permanently owned vehicle (except on a vehicle solely used for research and development), using trade licences on more than one vehicle simultaneously, keeping a vehicle displaying trade licences on the public highway, using a vehicle without displaying both current licences, or displaying licences that are altered, defaced or otherwise, and finally using a vehicle for any purpose other than those prescribed in the Regulations.

Licences are available for either six or twelve month periods, with fixed expiry dates of 30th June or 31st December. Adequate third party insurance must be effective during the use of trade licences. Passengers may be carried under trade licences, unless the vehicle concerned can carry only one person, and providing that the licences were obtained in connection with this purpose. Finally, trade plates cannot be used on a vehicle which is carrying passengers for hire or reward. The issue of trade licences does not allow passengers to be carried on a commercial basis.

## POSSESSION TAX - A NECESSARY EVIL ?

The closing months of 1994 saw the Government's Department of Transport produce a consultative document into a tax on vehicle possession. Designed as a means to crack down on road tax dodging which costs the Government over £145m per year, this tax would be levied on all vehicles even if they are not on the road. These plans would obviously affect those preservationists who only tax their vehicles for the six months of the year when rallies are held (generally April to October), as their vehicle would need to be taxed all year round. Also likely to be hard hit would be buses held as part of a museum collection, vehicles owned as a source of spare parts, or vehicles in dealers' or breakers' stock. The latter category could see historic vehicles being broken up rapidly rather than having to pay tax on them.

The Federation of Historic Vehicle Clubs is attempting to persuade the Government to apply an age limit to this legislation, which could exclude vehicles over 20 years old. Both the British Bus Preservation Group and the Historic Commercial Vehicle Society are monitoring the progress of this matter very carefully, and would-be preservationists would be well advised to consider the financial implications of acquiring a non-roadworthy bus or coach.

## *Chapter 11*

## GET OUT AND ABOUT !

Your shining exhibit by this stage will be fully roadworthy and legal and straining at the leash to transport you to the nearest rally field. The traditional rally season originally kicked off with the Cobham Bus Museum Open Day at the start of April and terminated with the Showbus event at the end of September (for many years this was held at Woburn Abbey, but from 1993 it is situated at Duxford in Cambridgeshire). However, today's rally season lasts for 365 days - there are even gatherings and events such as the Friends of King Alfred running day in Winchester which take place annually on January 1st !

Several events, typically those organised by large organisations such as the Historic Commercial Vehicle Society, take the form of a road run culminating in a static display at the ultimate destination. This format allows a large number of spectators the chance to see vehicles in action along the line of the route and also at the static exhibition. Perhaps the most famous of these events is the London to Brighton run, which has been staged on the first Sunday in May since 1962, and recent years have seen the legal maximum number of entries (180) taking part. In the north, the equivalent is the Trans-Pennine Run from Manchester to Harrogate. This event, which also attracts a maximum entry, started in 1969 and takes place on the first Sunday in August.

Events are usually publicised well in advance, and many will require an advanced entry application to be submitted. The magazines of the Historic Commercial Vehicle Society and the British Bus Preservation Group contain many of the details that you will require. Ian Allan's monthly periodical "Buses" has an annual summary in each April edition, and the classified columns of this journal contain more current details. Plan your schedule of appearances well in advance taking into account important factors such as travelling distance (not only for your fuel bills, but what if the bus breaks down on the rally field ?).

Try to attend those events which have a special significance to your vehicle, whether it be in an area where it once operated, a gathering of former members of a particular fleet, or a special event in your locality (eg a local operator's anniversary, etc). Make sure that your rally application is received by the organisers in good time for the event, as they may have to produce a programme (which will contain details of your vehicle) which may be printed well in advance.

Do not become limited to exhibiting only at bus and coach rallies, however. There are an infinite number of classic vehicle events staged for all manner of vehicles; preserved steam railway open days are often enhanced by the addition of a period bus; your local town carnival will probably be pleased to display a piece of the district's transport heritage - the possibilities are bounded only by your imagination !

It is helpful to the admission-paying enthusiast if you are able to display a little of the history of your vehicle somewhere nearby, perhaps mounted on a piece of wood or cardboard, or perhaps inside one of your vehicle's windows. Whilst some preservationists delight in answering the same questions all day long, an informative history summary will allow visitors to find information such as the chassis numbers for themselves - saving your voice and allowing you more time to do what you want to do ! Most organised rallies provide a free commemorative plaque for vehicle entrants: many vehicle owners will carefully affix this to an ornate display board, so as to compile a concise record of where the vehicle has been on display.

If you are particularly keen for your bus or coach to be judged as part of an event, it is useful to know what the judges will be looking for when comparing one vehicle with another. The following list details those areas which are always considered:

a)  Cleanliness of engine and all mechanical parts
b)  Cleanliness of bodywork - both internal and external
c)  paintwork, livery and insignia/transfers condition
d)  Equipment operation - mostly electrical accessories
e)  authenticity - proximity to original condition
f)  General appearance - judges' discretion applies

If you wish your vehicle to take part in classic bus journeys in conjunction with a rally or open day, then you should carefully consider the suitability of your arrangements before volunteering your services. Firstly, you should ensure that the vehicle will be driven by a person holding an unrestricted licence for the type that allows the carriage of passengers for hire or reward. Secondly, check that your vehicle has been tested to the required standard to legally carry passengers for hire or reward - at least a Class VI MOT will be required here. Your insurance cover should also be checked to ensure that it is in order for this type of usage, and amendments made if needed.

Most preserved vehicle owners, however, are happy just to drive their vehicles to and from an event, and display it for the enjoyment of interested members of the public during the intervening hours. It is a leisurely, casual pursuit where a vehicle owner can make many new friends and indulge in a little nostalgia and light-hearted rivalry - perhaps that is one of the reasons why it is attracting an ever-increasing number of new preservationists each year.

*Chapter 12*

# FOCUS ON VEHICLES

## 1. AEC ROUTEMASTER/PARK ROYAL

Introduced in the latter years of the 1950s, the well known AEC Routemaster with open rear platform Park Royal bodywork was built in great quantity for London Transport - 2760 RMs were completed by the time production ceased in 1968. They are extremely reliable vehicles with a rugged half-cab, bodywork format, and these two factors have lead to the survival of many of them today. Because of their reliability, those that are available for sale attract high prices from new operators outside of the Capital: consequently only a few cheap

*The Park Royal bodied AEC Routemaster was delivered to London Transport in a number of different formats. RML 2263(CUV 263C) is a 1965 example of the 30' chasis which seats 72, and is distinguishable by the small centre window. London Buses is currently refurbishing many of the remaining RMLs so that they will see service well into the 21st Century.*

examples are available for preservation. The standard length vehicle accommodates 64 seats on a 27' chassis, although longer 30' chassis (RML) derivatives could cater for 72 passengers. Coach seated RMC (standard length) and

RCL (extended length) versions offered a higher degree of comfort. Northern General took delivery of a small batch of front-entrance Routemasters in 1965, and BEA took similar forward-entrance versions (RMA class) in 1966/7 for connections between Central London and London Airport - these latter examples were equipped with their own trailers for the carriage of luggage. Most surviving Routemasters are currently receiving modern replacement engines (eg Iveco), and have lost some of their authenticity as a result. Despite their market price these popular vehicles are a good investment, and everyone will recognise the "traditional red London bus" !

Advertised examples - 1994

(i)      RM125 (VLT 125), hospitality unit, MOT, £8,000
(ii)     RM47 (VLT 47), AEC engine, £4,500
(iii)    RMC1497 (497 CLT), immaculate show condition, £12,000
(iv)     RM406 (WLT 406), AEC engine, in N Ireland, £5,000
(v)      RM1236 (MFF 579), recently withdrawn from London, £3,000

## 2. BEDFORD J2

The Bedford J2 was derived from the popular TJ-series truck chassis during the last few years of the 1950s. Powered either by a six cylinder petrol engine (J2SZ2) or four cylinder diesel unit (J2SZ10), the chassis was able to accommodate

*If vehicle size is a deciding factor when choosing a bus or coach, there are plenty of smaller alternatives readily available. XUM 123J is a 1968 Bedford with a 1970 Plaxton 16-seat body, restored in the livery of Worcestershire operator Hillcrest Radio Coaches of Alvechurch. Not only is storage easier to find for such a vehicle, but the low seating capacity means it can be driven on a conventional car licence !*

body-work of up to 20-seat capacity. Three main body types were fitted to the J2 - coach seated Plaxton and Duple (Midland) formats were popular with independent coach operators, whilst bus seated Willowbrook examples were taken into stock by the Ministry of Defence and Central Government. Their small size and relatively simple mechanics makes them an ideal choice for preservation, although examine the bodywork structure carefully for signs of corrosion and fatigue. Due to the J2 chassis continuing in use for lorries and horse-boxes, many Vauxhall/Bedford garages stock suitable spare parts. Not many of these remaining, however ....

Advertised examples - 1994

(i)     1963 Plaxton C18F, will MOT, used recently, £700
(ii)    Diesel-engined, Plaxton C20F, many new parts, £3,500
(iii)   1968 Diesel, 1970 Plaxton, will MOT, £700
(iv)    1969 Diesel, Plaxton, good cond, poss p/exchange, £4,000
(v)     1969 Willowbrook bodied, petrol, spares/repair, £100
(vi)    1966 Hawson B14F, new petrol engine, £750

## 3. BRISTOL LODEKKA

Bristol manufactured the Lodekkas during the 1950s and 60s as a standard double-decker for the state-owned bus sector. With all examples bodied by Eastern Coach Works (ECW) with a traditional half-cab design, early rear-entrance examples were known as the LD-series and these were superseded by the forward entrance FS and FLF-series in the early 60s, both of which had a flat floor. Mostly powered by five or six cylinder Gardner diesel units (the former option being slightly less powerful for operators in flat areas, but more economical) a few were delivered with Bristol engines and even fewer with the very favourable Leyland equivalent. The bodywork is very soundly constructed, and corrosion generally occurs only on a few examples around exposed areas such as the platform (LDs) cab floors and out-riggers (all types). Recent changes in the vehicles suitable for driver training duties have placed a lot of Lodekkas on the available list, and Top Deck Travel of Surrey still operate over thirty examples on inter-continental tours and expeditions, such. is their reliability. Many examples have been exported in recent years to destinations across Europe and America as tourist attractions - they are a cheaper half-cab alternative for use as a pseudo- London Bus than the genuine AEC Routemaster.

Advertised examples - 1994

(i)     Hants & Dorset Bristol FS6G, MOT, £2,000
(ii)    Ex Top Deck Bristol FLF6G, Caravan, no MOT, £1,000
(iii)   Ex Southern Vectis 1957 LD6G, MOT, £2,500
(iv)    VOD 503, ex Western National, converted to caravan, no MOT, £1,500
(v)     RAG 400, ex driver trainer, reasonable condition, £1,000

## 4. LEYLAND PD3

Leyland Titan production (of the front-engine variety) continued until 1969 when the last PD3 was produced. Bodied by a wide variety of manufacturers (Northern Counties, Park Royal, East Lancs etc), the majority were to a traditional half-cab design, and found much favour with the fore-runners of National Bus Company subsidiaries and municipal fleets alike. Southdown took several hundred PD3s in the 1960s which were unusual in being full-front examples bodied by Northern Counties. They are generally reliable with an abundant supply of spares still available. Their general ruggedness allowed many to survive as driver trainers until recently, and several continue to operate as open-toppers at seaside resorts around the country.

Advertised examples - 1994

    (i)      203 TTE, ex Lancaster, open-top, needs work, £475
    (ii)     Leicester 83 HBC (re-reg), East Lancs body, £1,500
    (iii)    Bournemouth 3913 EL, no stairs, £P.O.A.
    (iv)    Ex Blackpool LFR 538G, front damaged, £Offers
    (v)     MTJ 435C, needs work for MOT, £500
    (vi)    1966 Leicester, 8' wide, St Helens front, £1,000

*Recent years have witnessed a growth in demand for historic bus services. A new operator offering classic open-top journeys in West Sussex is Leisurelink of Crawley, who borrowed this 1956 former Southern Vectis Bristol Lodekka from a local preservationist for the 1992 season.*

## 5. AEC REGENT V

Between 1929 and 1968, AEC production at Southall produced the Regent as the main-stream double deck vehicle. Early Regents were basic petrol-engined vehicles, although the last release of the marque had evolved as the diesel-engined AEC Regent V of the 1960s. This type was preferred by many municipal fleets who ordered the vehicle by the dozen - they were typically bodied by Willowbrook, Park Royal, Massey, East Lancs etc. The Regent's AEC engines are fairly straight forward, and apart from the odd uncared for example, bodywork should not require too much attention. The Regent V is a plumber's nightmare if the water system requires attention, and the mono control gearbox is particularly complicated when it misbehaves. However, a good choice for an experienced preservationist.

Advertised examples - 1994

(i)   Ex Eastbourne 67 (KHC 367), MOT/COF, VGC, £3,000

(ii)  CTT 510C, Devon General, new MOT, exc cond, £1,200

(iii) Ex Trainer GJG 738D, good cond, MOT, £2,000

(iv)  Low bridge-bodied, ex Barton Transport, £Offers

(v)   Ex Maidstone & District, 1956 Park Royal, tax/MOT, £7,500

(vi)  1959, ex Hebble, restored, tax/MOT, £POA

*Southdown's infamous "Queen Marys" (Leyland PD3S with full-front Northern Counties bodywork) are currently much in demand by preservationists. The company, now part of the Stagecoach Group, has retained two convertible examples for preservation, including 409 (409DCD) seen in 1991.*

## 6. BRISTOL RE

A product of the 1960s that lasted until the mid 1970s was the Bristol RE. A full-size, horizontal, rear-engined, single-deck chassis was available in a variety of lengths for bodying either as buses or coaches, usually by Eastern Coach Works at Lowestoft. Many National Bus Company operators continued to specify the type for several years after 1970 in the same way as their predecessors had done before, due to the all-round proven versatility of the RE. Hundreds of examples were shipped to Northern Ireland when their usefulness in England expired, and there are many good examples available over the Irish Sea. As with the Lodekka, many received the reliable Gardner engine, although Leyland engined examples are still common. As bus companies modernise their fleets, REs are becoming increasingly more available to the preservationist - but beware, they need careful preventative maintenance to remain in good working order.

Advertised examples - 1994

(i)      Ex Southern Vectis HDL 23E, good condition, £1,850

(ii)     RELH6G reg XDL 122L, windows broken, £750

(iii)    RELH/ECW, W Yorks TWW 766F, will MOT, £1,400

(iv)    Bristol RELL, registration PYG 362N, £P.O.A.

(v)     Bristol RESL6G, TCD 481J and TCD 487J, scrap value, c. £500 each

*This Ipswich AEC Regent V is one a pair delivered in 1964 with unusual Massey bodywork. It is sadly no longer with us, however, after mechanical problems persuaded the owner to sell it abroad. It is now an immobile restaurant near Yokohama in Japan.*

## 7. BEDFORD EARLY SB-SERIES

The Bedford SB-series was a logical development in the 1950s from the ageing Bedford OB. It introduced forward control, where the driver sits alongside or forward of the front-mounted engine, and the early examples became standard coaches across the nation during the 1950s and early 60s. Available with either petrol or diesel engined power units, the stylish sweeping lines of bodywork such as that fitted by Duple enhanced the nostalgic appeal of these coaches with roof lights, wind-down windows, sliding entrance door and luxury seating. The SB series was continually standardised as time progressed, and the last examples produced in December 1986 possessed none of the style of the original members of that family. Maintenance is fairly straight forward on the uncomplicated mechanics, although the curved glass needed for roof lights, corner screens and windscreens on the elegant bodywork designs can be very difficult to locate or extremely expensive to re-manufacture.

Advertised examples - 1994

- (i)     Bedford SB, 1959 Yeates body, tax & MOT, re-reg, £1,500
- (ii)    Bedford SBG/1955 Duple Vega, needs restoration, £500
- (iii)   1958 Duple, ex Jennings of Bude, vgc, dry stored, £1,000
- (iv)    Bedford SB1, 1960, Yeates Europa body, £500
- (v)     Duple Vega, 97,000 miles from new, MOT, £Offers

*New to United Counties in 1968, this ECW-bodied Bristol RE was acquired by successor company Luton & District. It is currently officially preserved in the fleet, and occasionally sees service when not engaged on other special duties.*

## 8. LEYLAND ATLANTEAN

Leyland introduced the Atlantean chassis in 1956 as a planned successor to the front-engined PD-series Titans. The Atlantean was a rear-engined vehicle, with an entrance situated forward of the front axle, and the lack of a half-cab gave it a modern appearance for its time. However, it was not an instant success as many operators were reluctant to make a quick change to one man operation, a concept that was still in its infancy. The components of the 9.6 litre Leyland engine are bulky and access for servicing can be difficult, and the Leyland gearbox was often prone to problems. bodywork was supplied by a number of manufacturers, including Park Royal, Roe, East Lancs, Willowbrook, E.C.W. and M.C.W, and open-top and convertible formats were also constructed in quantity. Body corrosion is still comparatively rare as most specifications were constructed of aluminium. Several early examples are already preserved, and modern fleet replacement programmes are currently making many more available to preservationists.

Advertised examples - 1994

- (i)    Atlantean/Willowbrook, ex Brighton WUF 987K, £900
- (ii)   PBC 98G, ex Leicester, current MOT, £1,500
- (iii)  Ex Ribble NRN 599, 1960, exhibition unit, £2,800
- (iv)   EKD 431L, at Barnsley breakers, £Offers
- (v)    Convertible, 1961, with roof, no MOT, £600
- (vi)   MPJ 211L, MCW body, ex London & Country driver trainer, £2,500

*ODL 399, a 1957 Duple bodied Bedford SBG new to Moss Tours, Isle of Wight arrives in Ryde on a hydraulic suspended tow after nearly two decades of mainland operation. This coach was repatriated in two stages after being found near Worcester in 1992. Special arrangements had to be made to accommodate the combined vehicle length (over 55') on board Red Funnel's car ferry.*

## 9. AEC REGAL IV - LONDON TRANSPORT'S RF

AEC produced the single-deck Regent between 1929 and 1957, with the last four years production almost exclusively confined to export markets. The Regal IV, introduced in the late 1940s, drew on the Midland Red success of a sideways mounted underfloor unit which worked reliably. It also incorporated an air system for brakes, doors etc, and was able to be bodied in a number of different ways. London Transport took nearly 700 Metro-Cammell bodied buses and coaches (the latter including sightseeing vehicles with glass roof cants), whilst BEA at Heathrow employed a batch of Park Royal coaches with raised bodywork on their inter-terminal transport vehicles. Not surprisingly, there are several hundred RFs (as they were designated) surviving in preservation; parts are readily available, and providing the air system is sound, there should not be too many mechanical problems encountered. bodywork condition varies greatly depending on how well it has been looked after during its 40 year existence - there are some really nasty ones about !

Advertised examples - 1994

    (i)      Red LT RF463, near completion, needs painting, £1,000

    (ii)     Former LT RF512, needs much restoration, £800

    (iii)    Early Tourer, poor condition, stored for many years, £Offers

    (iv)    1953 RF + one other for spares, ex trainer, £3,750

    (v)     RF458 (MXX 435), very good condition, £4,500

*Leyland Atlanteans are gaining popularity amongst preservationists. This Park Royal Dual-door bodied example was new to London Country in 1972. The National Bus Company Livery which is carried is becoming a 'Historic' scheme since the effects of de-regulation in 1986.*

## 10. LEYLAND LEOPARD

One of the longest-lasting and durable British chassis was the Leyland Leopard which was introduced in 1959 and lasted 22 years until superseded by the Leyland Tiger in 1981. The under-floor Leyland engine (evolved from the Tiger Cub unit) generally proved to be extremely reliable, and the chassis was bodied by such companies as Plaxton, Duple, Willowbrook and Alexander. spares availability is very good, as there are still many examples which have only recently been confined to retirement in the scrapyard. A good all round coach for preserving, although it is a bit on the long side (up to 12 metres), and some preservationists consider this model to be too modern looking for a role in preservation.
Advertised examples - 1994

(i)     1968 Manual, Tax/MOT, Wheelchair Lift, £1,500
(ii)    217 CCH, Willowbrook body, ex Trent, £1,800
(iii)   Ex Rossendale Transport LTD 956F, £P.O.A.
(iv)    Plaxton Panorama I body, JVS 984D, £700
(v)     CAG 469C, Alexander body, needs seats, £Offers
(vi)    OUF 337J, ex Southdown, needs tidying, £900

*MXX 398, originally London Transport RF421, still sees occasional service with owner Autopoint of Hurstmonceux, Sussex. It is seen arriving at the Festival of Transport, Hellingly, in August 1991. During the early 1950's, London Transport took delivery of nearly 700 Metro-Cammell bodied AEC Regal IV's, of which many preserved examples survive.*

*Delivered new to Northern Scottish in 1970 was PRS 128J, one of an increasing number of Leyland Leopards finding a new home in preservation. This example now resides in South London, and the original livery enhances the historical appeal of this relatively youthful vehicle.*

# SPOTLIGHT ON SPARES

Membership of specialist societies such as the Historic Commercial Vehicle Society and the British Bus Preservation Group will supply you with newsletters and publications that will contain classified columns of spares available. A selection of assorted parts available in 1994 were as follows:

| | | |
|---|---|---|
| (i) | Leyland PD1 headlights, 1 pair, unused | £150.00 |
| (ii) | Morris (1920s) engine & gearbox | £450.00 |
| (iii) | Leyland Leopard gear selectors/forks | £ 40.00 |
| (iv) | Crossley dynamo, reconditioned | £ 65.00 |
| (v) | Bedford bus distributor, complete | £ 40.00 |
| (vi) | Bedford J2 petrol engine + 4-speed gearbox | £200.00 |
| (vii) | Albion Nimbus track rod and ends | £ 25.00 |
| (viii) | Bristol Lodekka - complete set of seats | £185.00 |
| (ix) | Foden bus manual - good condition | £ 45.00 |
| (x) | Leyland Atlantean body glass - from | £ 30.00 |
| (xi) | Duple Vega front indicator lenses, each | £ 15.00 |
| (xii) | Gearbox and axles for Daimler CVG6 | £250.00 |
| (xiii) | Hawson front wing indicator units, 1 pair, unused | £ 20.00 |
| (xiv) | Bristol KSW, bonnet top and side panels | £ 25.00 |
| (xv) | AEC Routemaster engine, from scrapped vehicle | £200.00 |

# *Appendix 1*

# UNDERSTANDING REGISTRATION NUMBERS

All vehicles used on the roads of Great Britain carry a number plate bearing a registration number. Whilst outwardly appearing to be a random selection of numbers and letters, this number indicates where a vehicle was originally registered (unless of course it has been re-registered), but may also give an indication of its age. The following sections detail how a number plate can be deciphered to obtain useful information.

## Registration Issue Codes

Registration numbers consist of a group of two or three letters, combined with one, two or three numbers. An additional single letter at the beginning or the end is a year indicator. Amongst the group of letters are a two character code which indicates where the vehicle was originally registered: for vehicles with three letters, the first character (which has no significance) should be disregarded. A list of such codes is detailed below.

| | | | |
|---|---|---|---|
| Aberdeen: | RS SA SO SP SS | | NS US YS |
| Aberystwyth: | EJ FF | Gloucester: | AD DD DF DG FH |
| Ayr: | CS SD SJ | Greenock: | VS |
| Bangor: | CC EY JC | Grimsby: | BE EE FU JV |
| Barrow: | EO | Guildford: | PA PB PC PD PE PF PG PH PJ PK |
| Birmingham: | DA JW OA OB OC OD OE OF OG | | PL |
| | OH OJ OK OL OM ON OP OV OX | Hastings: | DY HC JK |
| | UK | Haverfordwest: | BX DE |
| Bolton: | TD TE WH | Hereford: | CJ FO VJ |
| Boston: | CT JL | Huddersfield: | CP CX HD WE WF |
| Bournemouth: | EL FX JT PR RU | Inverness: | AS JS SK SS ST |
| Brighton: | AP CD FG HC NJ PM PN UF WV | Ipswich: | BJ DX GV PV |
| | YJ | Keith: | SE |
| Bristol: | AE EU FB HT HU HW HY OU WS | Kendal: | EC |
| Cambridge: | CE ER JE VA VE | Kingston-upon-Hull: | AG AT KH RH |
| Cardiff: | AX BO HB KG NY TG TX UH | Kirkwall: | BS |
| Carlisle: | AO HH RM | Leeds: | DN NW UA UB UG UM WW WX |
| Chelmsford: | AR EV HJ HK JN NO OO PU VW | | WY YG |
| | VX WC | Leicester: | AY BC CM FP JF JT JU NR RY UT |
| Chester: | CA DM FM LG MA MB TU | Lerwick: | PS |
| Coventry: | AC DU HP RW VC WK | Lincoln: | FE FW RE TL VL |
| Derby: | RC | Liverpool: | BG CM EM HF KA KB KC KD KF |
| Douglas (IoM): | MN | | TJ WM |
| Dudley: | DH DW EA FD HA NX UE WD | London: | GK GO HX JJ LA LB LC LD LE LF |
| Dumfries: | SM SW | | LH LK LL LM LN LO LP LR LT LU |
| Dundee: | ES SL SN SR TS | | LW LX LY UL X- (all except XP) |
| Durham: | BR GR PT UP | London Central: | HM HV JD LA LT LU UC UU UV |
| Edinburgh: | FS SC SF SG SX | | UW YE YH YK YO YP YR YT YU YV |
| Exeter: | DV FJ JY TA TT UO | | YW YX YY |
| Glasgow: | DS GA GB GD GE GG GM GS HS | London North East: | MC MF MG MH MK MM MU |

| | | | |
|---|---|---|---|
| London North West: | LA LC LF LK LO LP LR LW LX LY OY RK VB | Preston: | BV BY CK CW FR FV RN |
| London South East: | GU GW GX GY MX MY | Reading: | AN CF DP GM JH JM MO RD RX |
| London South West: | GC GF GH GJ GN GP GT | Salisbury: | AA CG HO LJ TR |
| Luton: | BH GS KX MJ NK NW RO RP TM VS | Selkirk: | KS LS SH |
| | | Sheffield: | AK DT ET HE KU KY WA WB WE WJ |
| Maidstone: | FN JG KE KJ KK KL KM KN KO KP KR KT | Shrewsbury: | AW NT UJ UX |
| | | Stirling: | LS MS |
| Manchester: | BA BN BU DB EK JA NA NB NC ND RJ TC VM VP VR VU VV | Stoke-on-Trent: | BF EH FA RE RF VT |
| | | Stornoway: | JS |
| Middlesborough: | AJ DC EF HN PY | Stranraer: | OS |
| Newcastle: | BB CN CU FT NL RG TN TY VK | Swansea: | CY EP TH WN |
| Newport (IoW): | DL | Swindon: | AM HR MR MV MW |
| Northampton: | BD NH NV VV | Taunton: | YA YB YC YD |
| Norwich: | AH CL EX NG PW VF VG | Truro: | AF CV GL RL |
| Nottingham: | AL AU CH NN NU RA RB RC RR TV VO | Warrington: | DJ ED JP TB |
| | | Wick: | SK |
| Oban: | SB | Worcester: | AB NP WP |
| Oxford: | BW FC JO UD WL | York: | BT DN HL JX VY WT |
| Peterborough: | AV EG EW FL | | |
| Portsmouth: | BK BP CR OR OT OW PO PX RV RX TP | Export Marks: | XP |

For example, a vehicle displaying JPF 103K was first registered in Guildford, Surrey: PS 1805 was registered in Scotland at Lerwick, and 23 ACD had a registration issued in Brighton.

## Registration Age Identification

The format of the number plate and the presence of a year letter will give an indication of a vehicle's age. The following section details the three different registration patterns.

*Format A - Registrations Issued Until 1964*

Vehicle registrations were made compulsory in 1904. Initial allocations to authorities included all single letters (not including I, Q and Z) and two letter combinations as far as FY followed by a number between 1 and 9999 (for example P 231, CD 7015). By the early 1930s, the available combinations of two letter registrations were diminishing rapidly, and 1932 witnessed the start of three letter issuing codes (by prefixing the issuing authority code with an additional letter) and a number between 1 and 999 (eg PPH 698, ODL 11). Some authorities used all of their allocation of this format, and then proceeded to reverse the characters (eg 379 BXM, 928 GTA). This format was first issued in 1953 in Middlesex, although it did continue in some locations until 1964 (Southdown Leyland Titans 400-424 DCD were issued in Brighton in 1964). A very few authorities even exhausted this format in the early 1960s, and they were forced to introduce two-letter reversals (eg 3535 PL, 386 DD).

As each authority was issuing registrations at a different rate, there is no visible age comparison between similar format registrations. So whilst the Kinrossshire allocation of SU 1-9999 was still being issued in 1963, Surrey had migrated through the three letter and three letter reversal stage, and was actively issuing two letter reversals !

SU (Kincardineshire) and SV (Kinrossshire), amongst other registration blocks, were never used to their full potential by their original issuing authorities, with the SU series only proceeding as far as BSU three-letter series and the SV block having never made it beyond the original two-letter series. In this case, those unused "dateless" marks (CSU to YSU and ASV to YSV series) have recently been made available by the D.V.L.A., and many preserved vehicles that have lost their original marks at some stage now carry such registrations.

*Format B - February 1963 to July 1983 Registrations*
Between the above dates, standard registrations (three letters followed by three numbers) were amended to incorporate a year suffix letter, which were changed on an annual basis. The respective year letters are detailed below (note the absence of I, O, Q, U and Z). For example,

| | |
|---|---|
| A -01.02.63 to 31.12.63 | M -01.08.73 to 31.07.74 |
| B -01.01.64 to 31.12.64 | N -01.08.74 to 31.07.75 |
| C -01.01.65 to 31.12.65 | P -01.08.75 to 31.07.76 |
| D -01.01.66 to 31.12.66 | R -01.08.76 to 31.07.77 |
| E -01.01.67 to 31.07.67 | S -01.08.77 to 31.07.78 |
| F -01.08.67 to 31.07.68 | T -01.08.78 to 31.07.79 |
| G -01.08.68 to 31.07.69 | V -01.08.79 to 31.07.80 |
| H -01.08.69 to 31.07.70 | W -01.08.80 to 31.07.81 |
| J -01.08.70 to 31.07.71 | X -01.08.81 to 31.07.82 |
| K -01.08.71 to 31.07.72 | Y -01.08.82 to 31.07.83 |
| L -01.08.72 to 31.07.73 | |

XUM 123J was registered in 1970 and FPT 590C in 1965.

*Format C - August 1983 to Current Registrations*
Since August 1983, the year indicator was prefixed to the front of the registration - a reversal of the established format. As before, year letters I, O, Q, U and Z will not be used. As can be identified from the following table, A 101 EPA was registered in 1983, whilst J2 DTS originated between August 91 and July 92.

| | |
|---|---|
| A -01.08.83 to 31.07.84 | H -01.08.90 to 31.07.91 |
| B -01.08.84 to 31.07.85 | J -01.08.91 to 31.07.92 |
| C -01.08.85 to 31.07.86 | K -01.08.92 to 31.07.93 |
| D -01.08.86 to 31.07.87 | L -01.08.93 to 31.07.94 |
| E -01.08.87 to 31.07.88 | M -01.08.94 to 31.07.95 |
| F -01.08.88 to 31.07.89 | N -01.08.95 to 31.07.96 |
| G -01.08.89 to 31.07.90 | |

# Exceptions to the Rule ......

However, there are a number of registrations used on vehicles in the United Kingdom that do not comply with the above logic. These are detailed separately below.

*Vehicles of Unknown Age*
When a vehicle is presented for its initial registration in this country, it will be allocated a year letter appropriate to its age. If its age is unknown, for example it has been imported from abroad

with no documented history, it will be allocated a year identifier prefix of "Q".

eg.     Q795 DPF - issued to a Bristol Lodekka of unknown age by the Guildford VRO in 1992

### Irish Registrations

Irish registrations traditionally utilise the letters "I" and "Z" with no apparent age identifier.

eg.     SOI 1234, EZH 45, MZ 300

Irish Republic registrations issued in the last five years or so consist of an age and location identification:

eg.     92 D 8003 - a Dublin mark issued in 1992
        93 C 2502 - a Cork mark issued in 1993

.... and this format is being applied retrospectively to vehicles which are being re-registered or imported into Eire:

eg.     66 D 2513 - a Dublin mark for an imported AEC Routemaster new in 1966

### Isle of Man Registrations

Registrations issued to vehicles on the Isle of Man consist of the letters "MAN" or have a location identifier of "MN". Recent issues have also been allocated year letter prefixes and suffixes, although the letters do not match those issued on the mainland !

eg.     MN 45      - 1963 Willowbrook bodied Leyland PD3
        MAN 10M - 1963 Willowbrook bodied Leyland PD3 (!)
        1053 MN  - 1974 Seddon Pennine IV

### Channel Islands Registrations

Guernsey registrations are purely numeric, and issued sequentially. Jersey issues are also sequentially numbered, but prefixed with a "J". Alderney registrations commence with the letters "AY". Sark, however, only permits vehicles of the horse-drawn variety, so no registration scheme is required.

eg.     35940      - Guernseybus Iveco 59.12 with Marshall body
        J 14672   - Leyland PD2 from Pioneer Coaches, Jersey
        AY 59      - Alderney registration on Sherpa minibus

### Military Registrations

Registrations displayed on active military vehicles consist of two digits followed by two letters followed by two digits. The letters indicate which Armed Force owns the vehicle.

eg.     12 RN 77  - a 1969 Bedford J2 used by the Royal Navy
        24 BT 12  - a Bedford SB3 used by the Army
        43 AC 71  - a 1966 Bedford used by the Royal Air Force

### Diplomatic Registrations

Vehicles used by diplomats in this country carry registrations of the following format: three numbers, "D", three numbers.

eg.  123 D 456

*trade plates*

Trade plates consist of three numbers followed by two letters - the characters are red on a white background. The letters show where the plates were issued, in the same way as standard registrations. Trade plates also carry a triangular licence showing their ownership details on one of the plates.

eg.     549 VU, 597 PF, 125 OI

## *Appendix 2*

# GOVERNMENT DEPARTMENTS & AUTHORITIES

## GENERAL

Department of Transport, 2, Marsham Street, London.SW1P 3EB.
Tel: (0171) 276 3000
D.V.L.A. Customer Enquiries (Drivers), D.V.L.A., Swansea SA6 7JL
Tel: (01792) 772151  Fax: (01792) 783071  Minicom: (01792) 782787
D.V.L.A. Customer Enquiries (Vehicles), D.V.L.A.., Swansea SA99 1BL
Tel: (01792) 772134  Fax: (01792) 782793  Minicom: (01792) 782756
D.V.L.A. Vocational Licence Section, D.V.L.A., Swansea SA99 1BR
Tel: (01792) 772151 or (01792) 783838

## TRAFFIC AREA OFFICES

EASTERN, Terrington House, 13-15, Hills Road, Cambridge. CB2 1NP.
Tel: (01223) 358922
NORTH EASTERN, Hillcrest House, 386, Harehills Lane, Leeds. LS9 6NF.
Tel: (0113) 2499433
NORTH WESTERN, Portcullis House, Seymour Grove, Manchester. M16 0NE.
Tel: (0161) 872 5077
SCOTTISH, 83, Princes Street, Edinburgh. EH2 2ER.
Tel: (0131) 225 1880
SOUTH EASTERN & METROPOLITAN, Ivy House, 3,
Ivy Terrace,Eastbourne, E Sussex. BN21 4QT.
Tel: (01323) 721471
SOUTH WALES, Caradog House, 1-6, St Andrew's Place, Cardiff.CF1 3PW.
Tel: (01222) 394027
WEST MIDLAND, Cumberland House, 200, Broad Streets, Birmingham. B15 1TD.
Tel: (0121) 631 3300
WESTERN, The Gaunt's House, Denmark Street, Bristol. BS1 5DR.
Tel: (0117) 9297221

# Appendix 3

## MUSEUMS, SOCIETIES & GROUPS

AEC Society (Miss L D Harris), 32, Kingscroft Road,Hucclecote, Gloucs. GL3 3RG

Alexander M-Type Society (Paul Nicholson), 49, Totland Road, Cosham, Portsmouth, Hants. PO6 3HS

Amberley Museum, Amberley, Nr Arundel, West Sussex. BN18 9LT.
Tel: (01798) 831370

Aston Manor Road Transport Museum, 208 - 216Witton Tram Depot, Witton Lane, Birmingham. B6 6QE Tel: (0121) 322 2298

Badgerline Enthusiasts Group, 30, Blandford Close, Nailsea, Bristol. BS19 2QQ

Bedford J2 Register, 47, Weldon Way, Redhill, Surrey. RH1 3QA

Belfast Transport Museum, Witham St, Belfast. Tel: (01232) 451519

Birmingham & Midland Museum of Transport, Chapel Lane, Wythall, Birmingham. B47 6JX
Tel: (01564) 826471

Black Country Museum, Tipton Road, Dudley, West Midlands. Tel: (0121) 557 9643

Bolton Transport Museum, Smithills Dean Road, Bolton, Lancs.

Bournemouth Heritage Transport, 17, Spetisbury Close, Bournemouth. BH9 3QU.
Tel: (01202) 537011 / 485837

Bournemouth Transport Museum. Tel: (01202) 590026

Bradford Industrial Museum, Moorside Hills, Moorside Road, Bradford, West Yorkshire.
BD2 3HP

Bristol Interest Circle (Allan MacFarlane), 18, Downs Cote View, Westbury-on-Trym, Bristol.
BS9 3TU. Tel: (0117) 9621573

Bristol Vintage Bus Group, 74, Ridgeway Lane, Whitchurch, Bristol.

British Bus Preservation Group (Chairman), 109, Wellington St., Peterborough, Cambs.
PE1 5DU. Tel: (01733) 898322

British Commercial Vehicle Museum, King Street, Leyland, Lancashire. PR5 1LE.
Tel: (01772) 451011

British Trolleybus Society, 2, Josephine Court, Southcote Road, Reading, Berks. RG3 2DG

Castle Point Transport Museum Society, 105, Point Road, Canvey Island, Essex. SS8 7TD
Tel: (01268) 684272

Channel Islands Bus Society, (Dr J R Young), Nottingham Polytechnic, Clifton,
Nottingham. NG11 8NS

Cheshire Road Transport Museum, Arley, Cheshire. CW9 6PD

Crosville Enthusiasts Club, (Mr J F Baker), Parkview, 13, Wepre Lane, Connahs Quay,
Deeside, Clwyd. CH5 4JR

Cumbria Transport Society (B K Pritchard), 1, Ling Beck Crescent, Seaton, Workington,
Cumbria. CA14 1EZ

Dewsbury Bus Museum, 7 - 11 Foundry Street, Ravensthorpe, Dewsbury. WF13 3HW
Tel: (01924) 497284

Devon General Society, 22, Newhayes Close, Exeter, Devon. EX2 9JL

East Anglia Transport Museum, Chapel Road, Carlton Colville, Lowestoft, Suffolk.  NR33 1BL
Tel: (01252) 518459

East Pennine Transport Group, 23, George Street, Lindley, Huddersfield, West
Yorkshire. HD3 3LY

Eastbourne Historic Vehicle Club, 37, Anderida Road, Willingdon, Eastbourne, E. Sussex.
Tel: (01323) 508963

Eastbourne Omnibus Society (John Bishop), 48, Bramble Drive, Hailsham, East Sussex.
BN27 3HA. Tel: (01323) 843202

Eastern National Preservation Group, 5, Barncombe Close, Thundersley, Benfleet,
Essex. SS7 4AQ

Edinburgh Transport Museum, Shrubhill, Leith Walk, Edinburgh.

Enfield & District Veteran Vehicle Trust, Whitewebbs Musem, Whitewebbs Road, Enfield,
Middx. EN2 9HW. Tel: (0181) 367 1898

Essex Bus Enthusiasts Group, 67, Perkins Road, Ilford, Essex. IG2 7NQ

Friends of King Alfred Buses (FoKAB), 71, New Road, Fair Oak, Eastleigh. SO5 7EN.
Tel: (01703) 695361
Glasgow & Clyde Valley Bus Preservation Group, 81, Glen Feshie, East Kilbride. G74 2BQ

Glasgow Museum of Transport, Kelvin Hall, 1, Burnhouse Road, Glasgow. G3 8DP.
Tel: (0141) 221 9600

Gloucester Transport Museum, Longsmith Street, Gloucester.

Go-Ahead Northern Bus Enthusiasts Association (GANBEA), 1, Regent Farm Court,
Henry Street, Gosforth, Newcastle-on-Tyne. Tel: (0191) 213 1157

Greater Manchester Trsnsport Society, Museum of Transport, Boyle Street, Cheetham,
Manchester. M8 8UW. Tel: (0161) 205 2122

Guy Owners Club, 73, Azalea Road, Blackburn, Lancs.

hastings RE Group, Park Cottage, Guestling, Hastings, East Sussex. TN35 4LT

Historic Commercial Vehicle Society (Chairman), Iden Grange, Cranbrook Road, Staplehurst,
Tonbridge, Kent. TN12 0ET

Hull Transport Museum, 36, High Street, Kingston-upon-Hull.

Ipswich Transport Museum, Cobham Road, Ipswich, Suffolk.

Keighley Bus Museum, c/o 29, Ethel Street, Keighley, West Yorkshire. BD20 6AN
Tel: (01535) 603379

Lincolnshire Vintage Vehicle Society, c/o 3, The Paddock, High Street, Skellingthorpe, Lincoln.
LN6 7TR. Tel: (01522) 689497

London Bus Preservation Trust, Cobham Bus Museum, Redhill Road, Cobham, Surrey.
KT11 1EF. Tel: (01932) 864078

London Omnibus Traction Society, Unit 8, Battersea Business Centre, 103-109, Lavender Hill,
London. SW11 5QF

London Transport Museum, Covent Garden, London. Tel: (0171) 836 8557

Maidstone & District and East Kent Bus Club, 42, St Albans Hill, Hemel Hempstead,
Herts. HP3 9NG

Manchester Museum of Transport, Queens Road, Manchester

Mersey & Calder Bus Preservation Group, 1, Vicar Road, Norton Tower, Halifax. HX2 0NL
Tel: (01422) 343557

Merseyside Transport Collection, Prince's Dock, Liverpool.

Midland Counties PSV Society, 16, The Avenue, Spinney Hill, Northampton. NN3 1BA

Museum of British Road Transport, Cook St, Coventry, West Midlands.

National Tramway Museum, Crich, Derbyshire. DE4 5DP  Tel: (01773) 852565

North Kent Vehicle Preservation Group, 42, Manor Way, Barnehurst, Bexleyheath,
Kent. DA7 6JN

North of England Open Air Museum, Beamish, Co Durham.  Tel: (01207) 231811

Omnibus Society, The Spinney, Meadow Road, Ashtead, Surrey. KT21 1QR

Oxford Bus Museum, Old Station Yard, Long Hanborough, Oxon.
Tel: (01993) 883617 / (01865) 400002

P.S.V. Circle, 10, May Close, Chessington, Surrey. KT9 2AP

Ribble Enthusiasts Club, 31, Ashworth Street, Waterfoot, Rossendale, Lancashire. BB4 7AY

Routemaster Heritage Trust. Tel: (0181) 398 0765

RT/RF Register (John Gray), 51, Chesterfield Road, Cambridge. CB4 1LN. Tel: (01233) 423487

Rushden Historical Transport Society, Old Railway Station, Station Approach, Rushden,
Northants. NN10 0AW

Sandtoft Transport Centre, Belton Road, Sandtoft, Nr Doncaster. Tel: (01724) 711391

Scottish Vintage Bus Museum, c/o 64. Primrose Place, Eliburn,
  Livingstone. EH54 6RW. Tel: (01506) 416364 / (01501) 40310

Sheffield Bus Museum (Mike Greenwood), 17, Willingham Close, Sothall, Sheffield. S19 6PD.
Tel: (0114) 255 3010

Southampton City Bus Enthusiasts (7164 Group), 16, Bassett Meadow, Bassett, Southampton.
SO1 7DY. Tel: (01703) 220317 / 790213

Southdown Enthusiasts Club, 43, Stone Cross Road, Crowborough, East Sussex. TN6 3DB
Southern Counties Historic Vehicle Preservation Trust, 74, Welland Road, Tonbridge,
Kent. TN10 3TB

St Helens Transport Museum, Old Bus Depot, 51 Hall Street, St. Helens. WA10 1DU.
Tel: (01744) 451681

Sussex Transport Interest Group, The Clubrooms, London Road Station, Brighton.
Tel: (01273) 306838 / 550780

Tameside Transport Collection, Roaches Industrial Estate, Manchester Road, Mossley,
Lancashire.

Telford Bus Group, 33, Linley Avenue, Pontesbury, Shrewsbury. SY5 0TQ. Tel: (01743) 790752

Transperience, Low Moor Site (Off Junction 2 M606), Bradford, W. Yorks

Transport Museum Society of Ireland, Howth Castle, Howth, Eire.

Transport Ticket Society, 4, Gladridge Close, Earley, Reading, Berks. RG6 2DL.

Welsh Industrial and Maritime Museum, Bute Street, Cardiff.

Wellingborough Vehicle Preservation Society, c/o 31, Melton Road, Wellingborough. NN8 1PU.
Tel: (01933) 228006

West Midlands Bus Society (Membership Sec), 41, Stonehouse Lane, Birmingham. B32 3DU.

West Midlands Vintage Vehicle Society, 99, Billesley Lane, Moseley, Birmingham. B13 9RB.

West of England Transport Collection, Winkleigh Airfield, Winkleigh.  Tel: (01392) 70895

West Yorkshire Transport Museum, Ludlam Street, Bradford, West Yorkshire.
Tel: (01274) 736006

Westside Enthusiasts Club (G W Bain), 12, Brisbane Street, Greenock, Scotland. PA16 8LN

Working Omnibus Museum Project (Clive Wilkin), 94, Kings Road, Cowplain, Hants. PO8 8UT.
Tel: (01705) 256602

# *Appendix 4*

## DEALERS & BREAKERS

Allco Passenger Vehicles, London.  Tel: (0181) 866 8900

Ted Brakell, Cheam, Surrey.  Tel: (0181) 644 9132

Tommy Goodwin, Carlton, Barnsley.  Tel: (01226) 752184

Alan Hardwick, Barnsley.  Tel: (01226) 727774

Carl Ireland, Hull, Humberside.  Tel: (01482) 342862

London Bus Export Co., Chepstow.  Tel: (01291) 689471

Norths, Sherburn-in-Elmet, N Yorks.  Tel: (01977) 682613

P.V.S. Carlton, Barnsley.  Tel: (01226) 722052

Geoff Ripley, Barnsley.  Tel: (01226) 727769

Smiths, Stratford.  Tel: (01789) 267990

Joe Sykes, Carlton, Barnsley.  Tel: (01226) 725702

Wacton Commercials, Bromyard, Worcs.  Tel: (01885) 482782

Wealden, Five Oak Green, Nr Tonbridge.  Tel: (01892) 836977

Whiting Bros, Ferrybridge, Yorks.  Tel: (01977) 674942

## *Appendix 5*

# COST OF THE FIRST YEAR OF OWNERSHIP

## GUIDELINES FOR COST CALCULATIONS

| | |
|---|---|
| Vehicle: | 1965 Bristol Lodekka, ECW 70 seat double deck body. |
| Acquired from: | Barnsley dealer. Last used by driving school. |
| Condition: | Sound. Some dented panels and missing seats and trim. |
| Price: | £1000 incl VAT. Missing parts available at extra cost. |
| Assumptions: | No major mechanical failure. No accidents. |
| | Vehicle restored and rallied during first year. |
| | Cost of restorer's own time and tools not included. |

| | £ | £ |
|---|---:|---:|
| **Purchase price** | | |
|   –   Phone call enquiries | 5 | |
|   –   Vehicle | 1000 | |
|   –   Replacement missing seats, spare tyre | 50 | |
| | | 1055 |
| **Journey to collect vehicle (100 miles away)** | | |
|   –   Travel outward to vehicle | 20 | |
|   –   1 day third party insurance | 10 | |
|   –   Diesel (£2.50 per gallon, 10 m.p.g.) | 25 | |
| | | 55 |
| **Restoration costs** | | |
|   –   Panels to be replaced (4 @ £15 each) | 60 | |
|   –   Window glass to be replaced (1) | 50 | |
|   –   Two replacement rear light clusters | 50 | |
|   –   Paint and undercoat (brush applied) | 200 | |
|   –   Specialist services (welding, etc) | 80 | |
|   –   Sundries (sandpaper, brushes, screws etc) | 100 | |
| | | 540 |
| **Legal costs** | | |
|   –   Class V MOT test fee | 35 | |
|   –   One year's fully comprehensive insurance | 220 | |
|   –   One year's PLG road fund licence | 130 | |
| | | 385 |
| **Ongoing costs** | | |
|   –   One year's open air storage, £10 p.w. | 520 | |
|   –   Diesel (as above, 1000 rally miles) | 250 | |
| | | 770 |

Maintenance costs

| | | |
|---|---|---:|
| - | One puncture repair | 30 |
| - | Sundries (bulbs, fuses, oil, antifreeze) | 90 |
| - | Replacement section of exhaust | 75 |
| | | 195 |

| | |
|---|---:|
| Grand Total for One Year: | £ 3000 |

Whilst the above calculation may appear to be a formidable outlay, bear in mind that the initial purchase price of the vehicle may well have increased significantly as a result of restoration costs and being returned to a running condition. In this example, the restored Lodekka was subsequently valued at over £2000, a 100% increase on the original value. The subsequent year's of ownership will cost much less than the first year detailed above, as the cost of buying and collecting the vehicle will obviously not be required, and the restoration costs should be very much reduced as this work nears completion. If the initial outlay is considered to be spread across the many years of ownership with a preservationist then the sums involved per year appear to be quite manageable.

# INDEX

## BRITISH BUS PRESERVATION GROUP

# THE BBPG IS A NATIONAL ORGANISATION WHICH IS DEDICATED TO THE RESCUING AND PRESERVATION OF BUSES.

In the past 5 years we have succeeded in saving more than 120 vehicles- some of which were hours from scrapping. We have over 500 members and offer the following -

**EXCELLENT BI-MONTHLY MAGAZINE**

**HELP WITH VEHICLE STORAGE**

**A SPARES SERVICE**

**A LIST OF BUSES FOR SALE**

**ANNUAL BUS RALLY VIDEOS**

In addition we have our own Bus Rescue Fund and have set up a National Bus Museum Building Fund

**Annual Membership is £12.00**
**(£7.00 unwaged)**

## Why not join us ?

send a 9" x 6" SAE to:

**Colin Temple**
**Membership Secretary**
**39 Tothill Road**
**Swaffham Prior**
**Cambridge CB5 0JX**